Praise for Steve Clarke

Excellent with lean manufacturing and kaizen. Awesome with streamlining the purchasing, distribution & planning functions, resulting higher inventory turns.

Roy Hendricks
Senior Buyer

Very knowledgeable in S&OP, ERP, Demand Management and business intelligence tools.

TEARRA KEATON
Supply Chain Manager

Very strong supply chain leader. Delivered strong customer service performance using lean methodologies.

JOHN BUCKLEY
Consumer Products Industry Advisor

Exceptional ability to bring multiple stakeholders to the table and persuade stakeholders to implement lean manufacturing principles. Great strategic vision.

Noel Fruchtenicht
Director, Supply Chain

He brought structure to the process and managed a very complex project in an incredibly dynamic environment.

Tobin Schilke
CFO

Re-built the supply chain processes which improved efficiency and reduced the operational churn.

Cliff Wylie
Senior Director, Supply Chain Planning

LEAN FORECASTING DEMYSTIFIED

LEAN FORECASTING DEMYSTIFIED

Steve Clarke

Copyright © Steve Clarke. All rights reserved.

No part of this publication shall be reproduced, transmitted, or sold in whole or in part in any form without prior written consent of the author, except as provided by the United States of America copyright law. Any unauthorized usage of the text without express written permission of the publisher is a violation of the author's copyright and is illegal and punishable by law. All trademarks and registered trademarks appearing in this guide are the property of their respective owners.

For permission requests, write to the publisher, addressed "Attention: Permissions Coordinator," at the address below.

Publish Your Purpose
141 Weston Street, #155
Hartford, CT, 06141

The opinions expressed by the Author are not necessarily those held by Publish Your Purpose.

Ordering Information: Quantity sales and special discounts are available on quantity purchases by corporations, associations, and others. For details, contact the author at steve@biosupplyconsulting.com.

Edited by: Brandi Lai, Connie Mayse, and Jill Kramek
Cover design by: Nelly Murariu
Typeset by: Jetlaunch

ISBN: 979-8-88797-115-5 (hardcover)
ISBN: 979-8-88797-116-2 (paperback)
ISBN: 979-8-88797-117-9 (ebook)

Library of Congress Control Number: 2024936687

First edition, September 2024.

The information contained within this book is strictly for informational purposes. The material may include information, products, or services by third parties. As such, the Author and Publisher do not assume responsibility or liability for any third-party material or opinions. The publisher is not responsible for websites (or their content) that are not owned by the publisher. Readers are advised to do their own due diligence when it comes to making decisions.

Publish Your Purpose is a hybrid publisher of non-fiction books. Our mission is to elevate the voices often excluded from traditional publishing. We intentionally seek out authors and storytellers with diverse backgrounds, life experiences, and unique perspectives to publish books that will make an impact in the world. Do you have a book idea you would like us to consider publishing? Please visit PublishYourPurpose.com for more information.

Table of Contents

Ch. 1, Waste Permeates Supply Chains Everywhere! 1
    My Background. 2
Ch. 2, The Eight Wastes of Forecasting. 7
    Defects 8
    Overproduction. 9
    Extra Processing 9
    Inventory. 10
    Transportation. 11
    Underutilized People. 11
    Motion 11
    Waiting 12
    Chapter Summary. 13
Ch. 3, A Cautionary Tale 15
    Night of the Long Knives 15
    3X Forecast Increase 16
    Mothers' Day Flowers 17
    Forecasts Are Important 19
Ch. 4, Balancing Demand and Supply 21
    Demand Planning. 23
    Supply Planning 24
    Capacity Planning. 25
    Strategic Planning. 27
    Sales and Operations Planning (S&OP). 28
    Master Production Schedule (MPS) 30
    Material Requirements Planning (MRP) 31
    Chapter Summary. 32
Ch. 5, Adding Value, Not Waste. 35
    Excessive Meddling. 35
    Forecast Value Added (FVA). 37

Arbitrary Targets 39
Demand Volatility 40
Demand Shaping 42
Chapter Summary 43
Ch. 6, Which Items to Forecast 45
When Less Is More 45
Convert Independent to Dependent Demand 47
Assemble to Order (ATO) 51
Pull Versus Push 52
Aggregation/Disaggregation 55
Chapter Summary 58
Ch. 7, Focus on Less! 61
ABC Item Stratification 62
Detailed Forecast Time Fence 63
Chapter Summary 66
Ch. 8, Select the Right Forecast Strategy 67
Demand Volatility 67
Demand Volume 68
High Variance, High Volume 70
High Demand, Low Variation 72
Low Demand, High Variation 76
Low Demand, Low Variation 80
Chapter Summary 83
Ch. 9, Executing the Forecast Strategy 85
Market Intelligence 86
Opportunities/Risks 87
Collaboration 89
Forecast Unit of Measure 90
Volume Versus Mix 91
Intervals 92
Time Horizon 94
Constrained Versus Unconstrained Forecast 95

Multiple Demand Sources 96
Chapter Summary. 96
Ch. 10, Balancing Forecasted and Actual Demand 99
Demand Control. 99
Available to Promise (ATP) 101
Capable-to-Promise (CTP) 103
Forecast Consumption 103
Customer Order Dates 110
Chapter Summary. 113
Ch. 11, Forecast Accuracy 115
Forecast Offset 117
Forecast Accuracy Calculation 123
Mean Absolute Percent Error (MAPE) 125
What is a Good MAPE? 126
Improving MAPE. 127
How to Convert Forecast Inaccuracy Data
to Safety Stock Levels. 127
Chapter Summary. 131
Ch. 12, Forecast Bias 133
Target Practice. 134
Positive Bias 136
Negative Bias. 138
How Do We Calculate Forecast Bias?. 139
Removing Bias 143
Chapter Summary. 143
Ch. 13, Optimizing Forecast Software 145
Garbage In, Garbage Out (GIGO). 145
User Requirements 146
Organizational Commitment 148
A Better Approach 150
Abnormal Demand. 153
Forecast Consumption Rules 154

Available-to-Promise (ATP) 154
Minimum Remaining Shelf Life (MRSL) 155
Dynamic Safety Stock. 156
Multiple Series 156
Chapter Summary. 157
Ch. 14, Case Study. 159
Background. 159
Define Excellence 162
Mine the Gaps 163
Ch. 15, Recap. 179
Defects 179
Overproduction. 181
Extra Processing 181
Inventory. 182
Transportation. 182
Underutilized people. 183
Motion 183
Waiting 184
Epilogue. 185
Competitive Advantage. 185
10 Takeaways. 186
Bibliography. 191
Recommended Reading 193
Acknowledgments 195
Index. 197
Types of Waste 201

Chapter 1

Waste Permeates Supply Chains Everywhere!

*Clutter and confusion are failures of design,
not attributes of information.*

—Edward Tufte, American statistician and professor

When I was ten years old, I went to work with my dad at a small clothing warehouse that he supervised. He gave me the particularly important job of counting labels for clothing items, which I performed diligently all summer long. One day, toward the end of the summer, I noticed a table against one of the walls. On the wall were markings in increments of one hundred. I asked him what they were for. He then divulged, with a sheepish grin, that they were a *slightly* easier way to count labels. He showed me how to stack the labels next to the marks so that you could quickly see how many labels were in the stack. In other words, he was telling me that all my manual counting was completely pointless!

Even at the tender age of ten, I had picked up a few cuss words at school. I didn't know what many of them meant, but I was very tempted to use them, though I wisely bit my tongue. Suffice it to say, I was a little annoyed. I can laugh about it now, but I still give my dad grief about it, even today. However, it taught me a valuable lesson about operational excellence. A simple tool like those markings could not only make a trivial difference but could also transform efficiency with no loss in accuracy. Even though he didn't know it, my dad was a Lean practitioner before anyone had coined the phrase.

This book is about applying that same principle to transform your sales forecasting process—not with expensive technology or a consultant in a fancy suit, but with **good, old, common-sense tools.** Over my career, I learned the power of this approach, and I have become a passionate advocate. In this book, I will share how to radically transform your forecasting process so it is more Lean, with far **fewer items** to forecast over a **shorter period of time.** Each new practice will include several stories and real-life examples from my thirty years of supply chain experience. Not only that, but I will also help you select the **right tools** so that your forecast errors shrink. You will learn which data to leverage to **accurately measure** your forecast accuracy. Finally, I will introduce some **controls** to prevent over-promising to your customers.

Your forecasts will never be perfect, but they will be much better than they are today. In short, I will show you how Lean Forecasting can transform your supply chain performance.

My Background

I have been reducing waste in supply chains for my entire career. It started after I graduated university in England and found my first professional job as a production planner for a medical device manufacturer. I was responsible for planning their radioactive product line with a sixty-day shelf life that could not be sold after thirty days. It was a global market, so we reconciled sales from multiple regions worldwide. The forecasts had an exceedingly small margin of error, with stockouts or expired inventory the penalty for getting it wrong. It was a baptism of fire, but I quickly learned how inaccurate forecasts can cause sleepless nights.

After all this time, I cannot deny that I am a geek when it comes to this stuff. In fact, I have taught Lean Six Sigma and APICS certifications for over twenty years to hundreds of students. I have now passionately removed waste in multiple industries, including medical devices, consumable products, agricultural chemicals, packaging, aerospace, biotechnology, and pharmaceuticals. I have worked for notable organizations such as Bio-Rad Labs, Jacuzzi Inc., Santen USA., BioMarin Pharmaceutical Inc., Danaher, PepsiCo Inc., and Bio-Techne. In addition, I have worked for much smaller organizations. In all these companies, large and small, one common denominator is that **waste permeates supply chains everywhere.**

My motivation for writing this book was to share what I find to be deeply gratifying. That is, an organization can take simple tools and practices and seriously transform its capability and performance. Global supply chain is a discipline that is pivotal in delivering products and services to customers everywhere, a discipline that employs millions of people who do not deserve the headaches and frustration associated with cumbersome, mistake-ridden processes. Headaches and frustration can arise any time our systems are not fit for purpose or we are working on dysfunctional projects that take priority over much more critical ones. Does this sound all too familiar?

It is frustrating to me that in some cases I waited twenty years to learn about new practices that turned out to be extremely beneficial. As I mentioned, I'm a geek and read about this stuff all the time. The fact that I had to wait so long to add something to my tool belt means that many supply chain professionals may go their entire careers without ever learning about these tools. This is what fueled my desire to write this book. So here we are. What better place to start than sales forecasts? Why? **Because all supply chains begin with knowing what the customer wants.**

In fact, the industry research organization Gartner[1] puts sales forecast accuracy at the pinnacle of its hierarchy of metrics, due to its criticality. Think about operational decisions and questions that all companies must make or ask at one time or another:

- ➤ What is our projected revenue this quarter?
- ➤ What will the expected month-end order backlog be?
- ➤ What is our projected quarter-end inventory?
- ➤ How much will we buy from Supplier A next year?
- ➤ When must we add more people or schedule overtime?
- ➤ When will we require more equipment, a new plant, a new office?
- ➤ When should we plan for additional warehouse space?

What do these questions have in common? Yep, they all require a sales forecast to effectively answer them.

---

1   Gartner, "Gartner for Supply Chain: Strengthening Supply Chain Performance Improvement Initiatives," Gartner (2021).

Thank you for choosing my book. I am confident that you will find it practical and valuable. Over my career, I have leveraged these tools and practices to successfully transform many supply chains. You will read about a multitude of these examples throughout the book. It is meant to be a practical guide to powerful proven practices.

Chapter 2

The Eight Wastes of Forecasting

Make everything as simple as possible, but not simpler.

—Albert Einstein, theoretical physicist

Those of you familiar with the Lean philosophy will know that it involves an organization intensely examining *how* it performs work with the intention of removing activities that do not add value. If it is not adding value, then it is waste. In assessing many business processes in different companies and industries, I typically find that at least ninety-five percent of activities do not add value. Even Toyota, the godfather of Lean, estimate that they still waste fifty percent of their effort on nonvalue-added activities. In other words, all organizations are target rich environments.

In Lean Forecasting, we define value as *actions that improve accuracy, with less effort.* In this way, you can better serve your customers with fewer stockouts. Any action that does not help achieve this objective is "waste," and you should remove it.

In the Lean philosophy, there are eight types of waste. Here is a quick overview of these wastes in the context of forecasting.

Defects

We define a defect as any time a product does not meet customer requirements. Does the customer want to pay for you to rework or scrap these defective items? Of course not. Even though they don't pay for every scrapped item directly, defects increase costs, so either you indirectly charge the customer or you reduce your profits. Obviously, neither scenario is desirable.

We can apply the same concept to defects created in the office, not just on the production floor. In the case of forecasts, defects refer to any time a forecast is different from actual demand. Those of you with some supply chain experience will know that **forecasts are always wrong.** Our job is to strive for the perfect forecast, knowing that it will never be achieved. Fewer defects translate to reduced inventory costs, expedites, scrap, lost sales, etc.

It is also important to understand that **there is a limit to forecast accuracy, given the demand volatility.** We will see the fallacy of the management team setting an arbitrary target based upon "industry benchmarks." Also, look out for any time executives meddle with the forecasts. This is especially true when they create bias in one direction or another. We will discover that there are ways the management team can support forecast accuracy improvements.

In addition, we will learn how to find the sweet spot between minimizing the number of forecasted items and maximizing forecast accuracy. Software configuration can also impact forecast accuracy through the management of forecast consumption and tracking demand spikes.

Finally, it is worth noting that it is very possible to have measurement errors. In other words, an organization may not use the right data for a calculation. This can lead to a wild goose chase while ignoring true forecast errors.

Overproduction

This waste is the mother of all wastes. It indirectly causes many other nonvalue-added activities, so it deserves special attention. Whenever we produce more than required, this is overproduction waste. The most egregious examples revolve around forecasting more items than necessary. We will discover how to avoid this type of waste.

Overproduction also rears its ugly head in several different forms. For example, suboptimal manufacturing strategies and inventory deployment often lead to excessive and unnecessary finished goods inventory. We will learn about the different approaches to mitigate this risk.

Finally, this waste category can also relate to user software requirements. Many times, when an organization announces a new software, people act like kids in a candy store and ask for everything but the kitchen sink. We will learn how to avoid this pitfall and properly prioritize requested functionality.

Extra Processing

Extra processing is primarily a result of rework, inefficient transactions, or inappropriate strategy. In the context of forecasting, rework is frequently created when the initial forecast is missing critical data (e.g., insufficient time horizon). Then planners must rework the forecast to render it fit for purpose. This waste could result from unnecessary adjustments to the forecast. A number of studies have shown that these changes create more forecast errors. In Jonathon Karelse's 2019 article on improving forecast performance, he describes how a study conducted by NorthFind Management found that nearly ninety percent of demand planners tended to consistently over (or under) estimate in one direction—and that forecasting performance was often significantly impacted as a result.[2]

Extra processing may also result from the selection of the wrong forecast strategy, given demand volume and volatility. We will learn how to select the proper strategy based on an item's demand profile. Finally, as we will see later, extra processing could be due to nonuser-friendly software that requires workarounds due to functionality gaps.

Inventory

Forecasts can be a primary cause of excess product inventory. Insufficient consideration for demand or lead time volatility can result in suboptimal safety stocks and overflowing warehouse racks. We will learn how to optimize inventory to minimize this waste. We will also learn about how "push" systems tend to create more inventory waste than "pull" systems.

---

2   Jonathon Karelse, "How to Improve Forecast Performance by Reducing Human Bias," LinkedIn (2019).

Transportation

In this context, transportation refers to excessive hand-offs built into the design of the forecasting process. For example, when an organization requires multiple approvals, this constitutes transportation waste. In addition, when people work in multiple discrete electronic files instead of a shared file, think of these files as cars that travel across the globe between inboxes. Then, you can appreciate how much more travel is involved with discrete versus shared files.

Underutilized People

Whenever we disempower employees from using their brains, skills, and knowledge, we create regrettable waste. For example, I have often seen the knowledge of demand planners be ignored because their information contradicts a message that management wishes to send. Maybe it is clear that demand for a new product is not living up to the hype, but the sales team is not prepared to admit "defeat" yet. In addition, this could also happen when we do not share valuable information related to future demand, including information held by the customer. We should also consider it wasteful if we fail to capture data accurately or at all. We'll review practices to better formalize the sharing of this critical information.

Motion

In this case, motion refers to excessive effort required in the forecasting process. If we spend more time on low demand items than they warrant or need, that is wasteful motion. You will learn about how ABC stratification—categorizing products by value—will separate the "critical few" items from the "trivial many," so your organization has a sharp focus on the right items. Motion also refers to forecasts at unnecessarily low levels in the product hierarchy, requiring more effort than necessary, without any improvement in forecast accuracy. To remedy this waste, I'll introduce the concept of **aggregation**, which will provide a structured approach to the selection of the optimal level of the hierarchy to develop your forecasts.

Waiting

There are multiple reasons for delays in the forecast process, and each one creates waste. These reasons include delaying our response to forecast errors or waiting for all demand sources. Waiting could also include any time we do not complete key strategic actions in a timely manner, thus hindering the forecast process. I will introduce the concept of **demand control**, which provides a formal process for rapid identification and resolution of forecast errors.

Now, we understand more about the different waste types possible within the world of forecasting. As mentioned earlier, the perfect forecast is unrealistic, but a markedly better forecast makes everyone's lives so much easier.

Chapter Summary

This chapter covered the eight wastes of Lean and how they apply to the forecasting process. Here are examples of each:

- ➤ **Defects:** forecast inaccuracies
- ➤ **Overproduction:** the forecasting of too many items
- ➤ **Extra processing:** forecast rework due to missing demand sources in the original forecast
- ➤ **Inventory:** sub-optimal safety stocks since demand variation is not considered
- ➤ **Transportation:** excessive handoffs in the development of forecasts each month
- ➤ **Underutilized people**: ignoring demand planner input in the published forecast
- ➤ **Motion:** expending too much effort on forecasting items with low demand and low demand volatility
- ➤ **Waiting:** not reacting quickly enough when actual demand is significantly different than forecasted demand

Chapter 3

A Cautionary Tale

Prediction is very difficult, especially if it's about the future!

—Niels Bohr, Danish physicist

Night of the Long Knives

I came into work one morning to learn that most of the senior management team had been fired. In the following few months, everything was different at the company where I had worked for five years. The most tangible change was that the company closed the plush corporate office where I had worked. They gave me a choice: relocate to the manufacturing site or adios. Given that I had a wife and three kids settled in a lovely small town on the water, with many good friends, there was no desirable choice. In the end, we reluctantly relocated from the San Francisco area to be close to the manufacturing site in Southern California.

One of the key reasons we decided to move was that the company, which had previously been hemorrhaging cash (hence the firings), had just acquired a major new customer. This account promised to be the savior of the company with one-thousand stores across the country. In fact, the sales team projected that this new customer would increase our total revenue by thirty percent. As you can imagine, there was a new excitement and positivity that had been missing for some time.

On my last day at the old office, the CEO shouted after me, "Don't screw it up!" as I packed my belongings. Since I headed the US Supply Chain organization, it was my responsibility to ensure that the new customer got everything it needed, on time and in one piece. No pressure, right?

Everything worked well for several months. Then, one day, the sales team sent me an updated forecast as they did at the start of every month. Typically, I would start by quickly scanning the new numbers to see if any of them stood out. There would be some minor changes, but nothing to get excited about. Not this time! I will not repeat the words that instantly left my mouth.

3X Forecast Increase

Bill was the sales manager for the new account, and he had suddenly tripled his unit forecast starting in two months for one of the major product lines. We manufactured and marketed ceramic products for the bathroom (i.e., toilets, sinks, etc.). In other words, production output would also need to triple very quickly to meet this enormous increase. Was he smoking something? I gave him a call, and he confirmed that the numbers were accurate. It was a promotion he had been working on for some time, but he did not want to say anything until he had sealed the deal. Thanks, Bill! I knew this would be the start of a long few months, as we worked tirelessly to quickly achieve a three-hundred percent increase in production.

After I picked myself up off the floor, I dusted myself off and tried to think. We had outsourced this product to a contract manufacturer in Colombia. Their standard lead time was three months, and this did not account for the four-week transit time to the US. I knew my bosses would not receive the news well if I told them that tripling production in the time required would not be possible. Even though it was incredibly bad communication from the sales team, management would still expect the supply chain group to deliver. Put it this way: the company had not yet onboarded the notion of *Don't shoot the messenger.* This was especially true in this case due to our financial challenges at the time.

Knowing that "no" was not an option, the only solution to this massive challenge would be to import products by air instead of ocean. This would trim the transit time from four weeks to two days. As you can imagine, given the bulky nature of the product line, the elephant in the room was the cost of this alternative shipment mode. It would be several times more expensive, but we had no choice. So, that is what we did. We contracted with an airline and chartered planes to import the products from Colombia to the US. If this sounds like an episode of *Narcos*, the thought did cross our minds that this could look like suspicious activity.

Mothers' Day Flowers

For several weeks, it seemed that we had dodged the bullet, and we were able to deliver on time. That was, until I received the email:

Dear Mr. Clarke,

Thank you so much for your business. We regret to inform you that there will not be any aircraft available for the next few weeks. At this time of year, we allocate all our aircraft for importing roses into the country for Mother's Day.

Regards,

Joe

I can still remember the gut-wrenching feeling. I knew that the precious new customer could well be out of stock for its huge national promotion within the next couple of weeks. This would be a prime example of screwing it up. When I read that the reason for the aircraft shortage was due to doting children and husbands buying flowers for Mother's Day, I didn't know whether to laugh or cry.

My first instinct was that I should update my resume. My next thought was, how could I explain this to my family? "Hey guys, you know how I just uprooted your lives for my job? Oh, and not to mention that you left all your friends behind. Well, funnily enough, they just fired me, so all the upheaval was for nothing. Life is funny sometimes, isn't it?" My wife would be more understanding if I explained that it was for a worthy cause. But then again…

Fortunately, however, we were able to persuade the contract manufacturer to temporarily raise their capacity, which somehow just kept our heads above water. My worst fears did not happen, and I retained my job. In fact, we recovered so well that we received a commendation from the customer for our outstanding delivery performance. Thankfully, they could not see behind the curtain.

Forecasts Are Important

The reason I tell you this story is not just because it is quite amusing (at least, in retrospect), but also to highlight that forecasts are important. In fact, in his 2017 paper "Win the Business Case for Investment to Improve Forecast Accuracy," Gartner Practice vice president Steve Steutermann found that for every one percent of forecast accuracy improvement, companies on average realized gains including seven percent reduction in finished goods inventory, two percent reduction in transportation costs, and a nine percent reduction in inventory obsolescence.[3]

Just think about how important forecasts are in everyday life:

➤ We get wet when it rains unexpectedly.

➤ We go broke if we spend more than we budgeted.

➤ We lose savings if the stock that we fancied turns out to be a dud.

➤ We become sick if approved medications do not work as predicted.

➤ We wait at traffic lights if traffic flow in the city center is not as projected.

The bottom line is that terrible things happen when the crystal ball breaks. Even though they will never be perfect, there are many ways that we can make forecasts better align with reality.

---

3 Steven Steutermann, "Win the Business Case for Investment to Improve Forecast Accuracy," Gartner, 2017.

Chapter 4

Balancing Demand and Supply

There are dreamers, and there are planners; the planners make their dreams come true.

—Edwin Louis Cole, American missionary

By now, you will have gotten my point that demand planning is a critical function within the supply chain world. So far, we have explored how to streamline the process and make it more accurate, simultaneously. In this chapter, we will zoom out and consider where demand planning sits in relation to supply planning. As we will find, demand planning is nothing without its partner, supply planning. They are not always in harmony, but life is so much better when they are in balance. Therefore, it is important that I introduce both the yin and the yang.

The diagram below illustrates how we can connect demand and supply planning in the supply chain planning process. Note that there are three columns on this diagram: demand planning, supply planning, and capacity planning.

Lean Forecasting Demystified

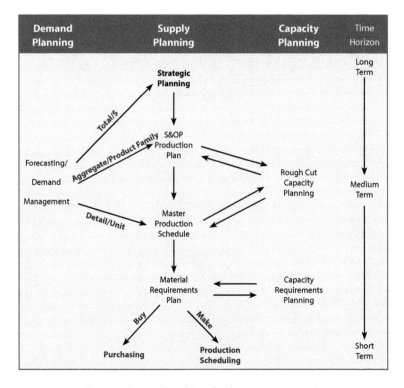

Figure 1: Demand and Supply Planning Framework.

We will now break this diagram down by column to see how everything is related to each other, starting with demand planning.

Balancing Demand and Supply

Demand Planning

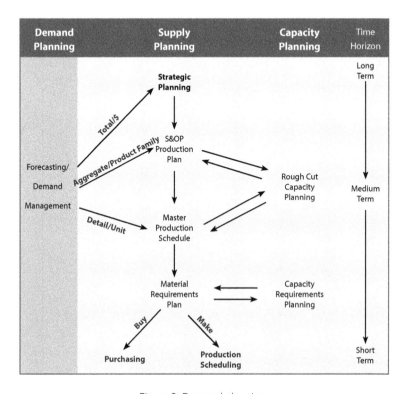

Figure 2: Demand planning.

Demand planning is the primary input to supply planning. The demand plan will either be at the business unit, product family, or individual stock- keeping unit (SKU) level. The level of detail becomes higher as we descend the planning hierarchy. The higher levels will be more focused on revenue, whereas lower levels will be focused on the unit level.

Supply Planning

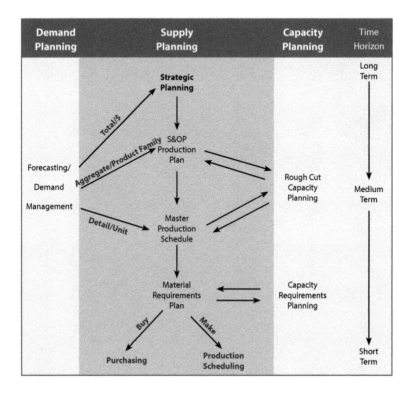

Figure 3: Supply planning.

The primary objective of supply plans is to fulfill the demand plans. The supply planning process will always seek to remove imbalances with the demand plan. For example, if demand becomes heavier, then the system will recommend more planned supply orders to redress the balance. Conversely, a lighter demand will mean that the system will plan less supply. In a perfect world, suppliers have infinite capacity and can always fulfill demand. But as we all know too well, this is not always the case. Just like any relationship, misalignments occur, and demand and supply become imbalanced. Why? Obviously, supply capabilities are finite, which is where capacity planning (right column) comes into play.

Capacity Planning

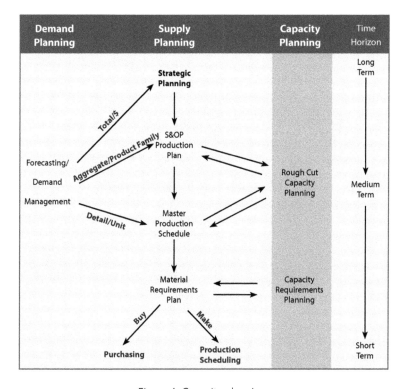

Figure 4: Capacity planning.

The purpose of capacity planning is to keep things real. Once we reach supply capacity, we can only support additional demand with more capacity, such as weekend work, the acquisition of more equipment, etc.

Now that we have moved horizontally from left to right, we will move vertically from top to bottom. Note that as we move downward, the time horizon becomes shorter, and the plans become more detailed. You may ask, *Why not just have a detailed, short-term plan and bypass all the other planning levels?* I'm glad that you asked! It is like spending all your money on short-term entertainment, toys, vacations, etc. and not paying attention to the fact that your house will soon need a new roof and the kids will want to go to college eventually. In the supply chain arena, we may require a new manufacturing plant to keep up with demand. In some regulated industries, these plants can take years to build and obtain approval. Planning requires a good balance between demand and supply, in addition to a balance between long-term and short-term needs.

Balancing Demand and Supply

Strategic Planning

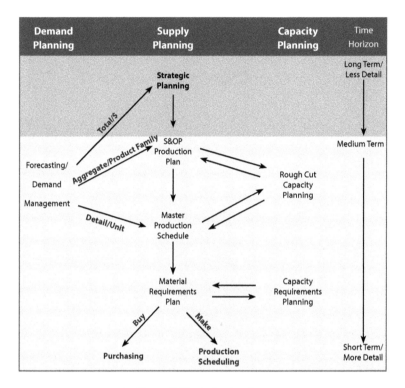

Figure 5: Strategic planning.

Strategic Planning has a time horizon of about five years. Discussions at this stage will include new product families, discontinuing products, new plants, offices, warehouses, etc. At this level, we focus the demand forecast on value, not units.

Using the household analogy again, this would be akin to discussions about how many more kids do we want and how many bedrooms the new house will require.

Sales and Operations Planning (S&OP)

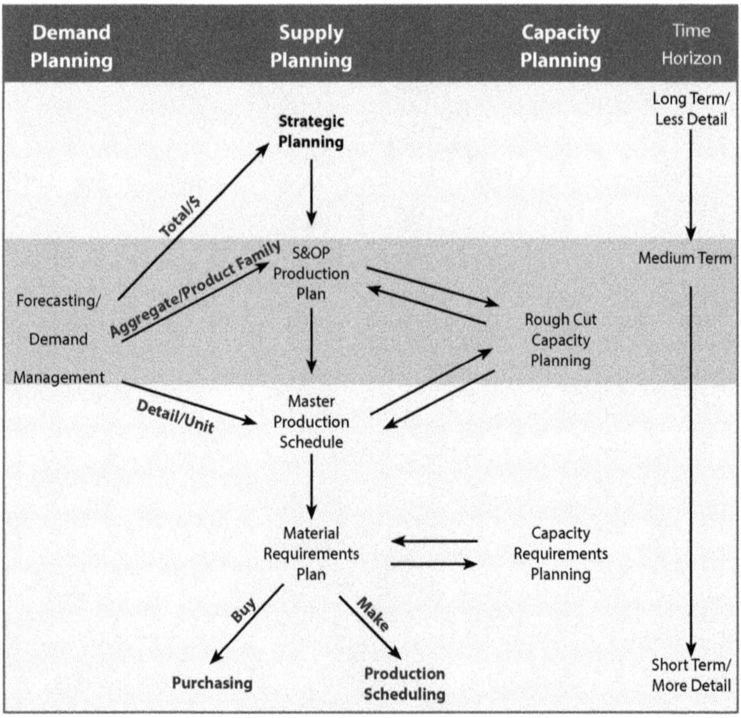

Figure 6: Sales and operations planning.

The next level down is the sales and operations planning process. The planning horizon for this process is eighteen months. Demand forecast is at the product family level. In other words, we will not forecast the mix here, but instead the unit volume for each product family.

For example, planners in the automotive manufacturing industry could project the total volume of each model that they expect to sell each month. This is enough detail to make decisions regarding capacity, hiring, budgets, etc., but not enough detail to schedule production or to know which materials to order. In the case of household planning, this is like asking if we are going to take a vacation in Hawaii this summer or just drive up to stay with the grandparents. How much will Johnny's college cost, and will that old fence withstand another winter?

We will perform rough cut capacity planning (RCCP) at this level. RCCP starts with critical resources within a bill of resource (BOR).

For example, say that highly skilled production workers were a critical resource, and your production plan called for one-thousand units of a particular product family. If the BOR called for four labor hours per unit, then it is a simple calculation to estimate that we would require about four-thousand labor hours that month. The BOR can also include equipment, materials, and logistics resources, etc.

Master Production Schedule (MPS)

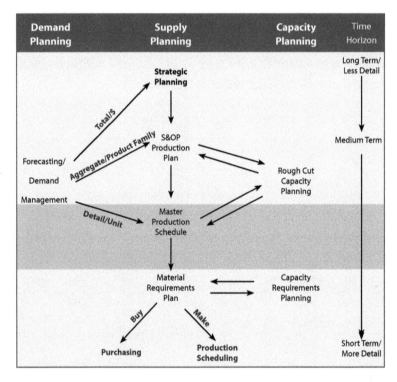

Figure 7: Master production schedule.

It is in the next level, master production schedule (MPS), that we create plans for individual SKUs. The time horizon will depend upon the cumulative lead time required to purchase materials and manufacture the product, otherwise known as the planning time fence.

At the household level, it could be that you have finally decided to replace that rickety, old fence, but you will need to wait a couple of months for the wood to arrive. You will build it yourself with help from friends, but they will not be available for several weeks after the wood arrives.

RCCP is also the capacity planning technique at the MPS level. However, since the MPS is at the detailed product level, it is no longer necessary to calculate average resource requirements in the BOR.

Material Requirements Planning (MRP)

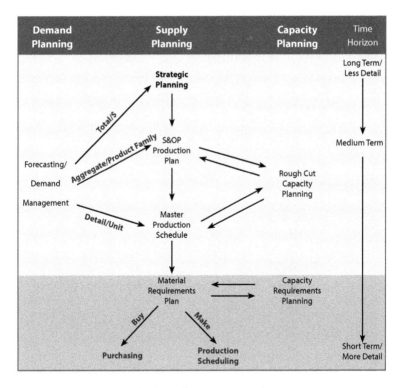

Figure 8: Material requirements planning.

Finally, material requirements planning (MRP) is typically where we plan components and materials, which could be "buy" or "make" items. The MPS is the primary driver of demand for these items, along with the bills of materials (BOMs)—the "recipe" containing all the ingredients and quantities required to build each master scheduled item.

Detailed capacity planning, known as capacity requirements planning (CRP), is the last level of this process. Organizations struggle with CRP due to the number of data inputs they need to maintain to generate accurate CRP outputs.

For example, an organization using CRP must maintain accurate work center data, routings, operation level schedules, production orders, and item masters. I would try to avoid this process unless it is absolutely necessary and your team has an elevated level of maturity when it relates to this data management.

Chapter Summary

> **Achieve demand and supply planning** balance at all times.

> **Demand plans** can be in terms of revenue, product family, or detailed units to support the various levels of the planning process.

> **Supply plans** seek to meet the demand plans, but capacity constrains them.

> **Strategic plans** look ahead five years, whereas S&OP plans for the next eighteen months require MPS for the cumulative product lead time, and the MRP horizon

Balancing Demand and Supply

should stretch through the lead times of both suppliers and manufacturing.

➤ **Capacity planning,** which uses the RCCP process at both the S&OP and MPS levels, focuses on critical resources. Companies leverage CRP at the MRP level and require many more data inputs than RCCP.

Chapter 5

Adding Value, Not Waste

Success is on the far side of failure.
—**Thomas J. Watson, Former CEO, IBM**

Excessive Meddling

On July 25, 1976, the Viking 1 orbiter took a photograph of the Martian surface that included a formation resembling a face-like structure.

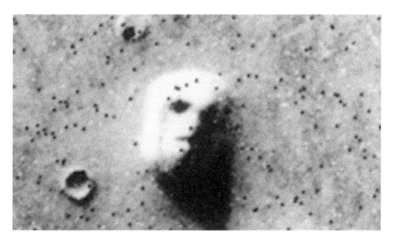

Image 1: Surface of Mars as seen from NASA's Viking 1 Orbiter spacecraft. "Geologic 'Face on Mars' Formation," July 25, 1976.

The photo created quite a stir back on Earth with rumors that the face was evidence of life on Mars and that NASA was covering it up. Since then, it has been featured on radio shows, talk shows, tabloid papers, books, and websites. Personally, I tend to lean towards NASA's explanation that this was an example of pareidolia, a psychological phenomenon where the human mind perceives familiar patterns, shapes, or meaningful images in random or ambiguous stimuli. Their caption below the photo read: "The huge rock formation in the center, which resembles a human head, is formed by shadows giving the illusion of eyes, nose and mouth."

Forecasters suffer from the same illusions. As human beings, we are exceptionally good at finding structure and pattern in the world around us—even when none exists. We overreact to each snippet of information. We tend to make changes to forecasts when the best course of action is to do nothing. Humans tend to be optimistic and underestimate future uncertainty.

Many times, people have an agenda, whereas calculations do not. When management defines annual quotas, suddenly, salespeople become very conservative to give themselves easier targets. When an organization launches a new product, marketing might exhibit "irrational exuberance." Worse still, all this executive meddling can get expensive quickly. The statistical approach is much more efficient. Whenever a judgmental override like this happens, record it as a separate forecast and compare their accuracy to quantitative methods.

There is nothing inherently wrong with having a version of the forecast with the purpose of driving the sales team. However, do not confuse this forecast with the "best guess" version. I have often experienced situations where executive management provides a top-line revenue target, and it is then the job of the demand planning team to determine the product mix to match the target. It is best to capture this executive management version of the forecast but to drive the supply chain based on a more data-driven approach.

Forecast Value Added (FVA)

As we know, the Lean approach is all about differentiation of value-added activities versus waste. Value-added activities are those that the customer is willing to pay for, and all the rest are known as waste.

Forecast value added (FVA) is a tool to measure the value of all the organizational effort spent on developing the forecast. FVA analysis starts with a "naive" forecast—that is, a forecast created by simple means that takes no time at all. The most common approach is to take last month's demand and use it as the forecast. Alternatively, in an environment with seasonal sales, the forecast could be the actual demand from the same month last year. The difference in accuracy between your published forecast and the result of a naive method is how we calculate the value added by your efforts.

If your forecasting efforts are not better than the naive forecast, then you may want to rethink your approach. You may scoff at such a thought, but the naive forecast can be surprisingly difficult to beat. Obviously, if your naive forecast is better than your published forecast, then your current process is adding negative value and is completely wasteful.

Similar to the Hippocratic Oath, the duty of the forecaster is to "first do no harm." In this context, that means ensuring that your work is not making the forecast worse. If you do not understand the accuracy of the "effortless" approach to forecasting, it is impossible to know whether your forecasting efforts are value-added or not. Clearly this must be our first step. We can call this the "baseline" accuracy level.

It is also a good practice to measure FVA after each step of the forecast process.

Figure 9: Simplified forecasting process.

In the example above, you first develop a statistical forecast. Next, the sales team makes modifications based upon market intelligence, and finally, the VP Sales reviews the forecast and usually also makes alterations. It would not be surprising to learn that the original statistical forecast was the most accurate. It is typical that human intervention creates more inaccuracy. By tracking the forecasts at each of the three steps, you will soon discover the FVA at each step. Based upon the results, we can make recommendations to the executive team in terms of process reengineering to optimize both accuracy and efficiency.

Arbitrary Targets

In 2004, director James Cameron said, "Hope is not a strategy" when addressing the NASA Administrator's Symposium.[4] He was referring to his exploration of the Titanic wreck, to which he has made thirty-three dives. Suffice to say, hope did not play a large part in his planning process. In fact, his engineering team spent seven years building the submersible capable of performing this feat.

I mention this anecdote because I have worked in many organizations that create arbitrary targets for forecast accuracy. Management sets these targets and insists that forecast accuracy gets better. They do not seem to realize that there is a strong inverse relationship between the volatility of a demand pattern and our ability to forecast accurately. As the diagram below shows, more demand volatility results in lower forecast accuracy.

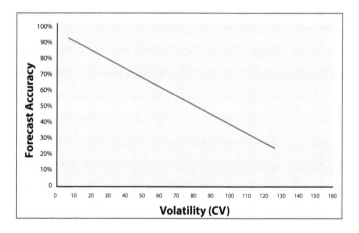

Figure 10: Relationship between volatility and forecast accuracy.

---

4 Steven J. Dick and Keith L. Cowing, ed., "Risk and Exploration: Earth, Sea and the Stars," NASA Administrator's Symposium (2004), 128.

Instead, they look for state-of-the-art software that is going to magically calculate super accurate forecasts. Do not fall for it. This is a foolish approach and destined to end badly. Equally unadvisable is to compare forecast performance to industry benchmarks. Since we do not know the volatility level of demand within other organizations, we cannot perform a fair comparison. The bottom line is that we cannot wave a magic wand and *hope* that those developing the forecast can consistently predict demand despite all this volatility.

Demand Volatility

Demand volatility is typically measured using the coefficient of variation (CV). It indicates whether a demand pattern is stable—staying close to its average value—or is highly unpredictable. CV is simply the standard deviation of demand divided by average demand. If only we could reduce volatility, we could improve forecast accuracy. You do not necessarily need to live with the current volatility level.

However, I have good news—not all volatility is necessary. It is important to understand that there are two types of volatility: **inherent and artificial**.

Inherent volatility is the natural variation of demand by consumers, and we typically have no control over this. However, **artificial volatility** is when shipments throughout the supply chain are more erratic than the inherent variation. For example, when a manufacturer ships its products to a distributor, they typically have a much higher CV than the inherent volatility. Here are some explanations:

➤ Shipping cost reduction: Larger loads are less expensive per unit. For bulky items, this could be a major consideration.

Potential solution

If your organization has several customers in the same region, change the sales terms so that you become responsible for freight costs and then consolidate shipments to customers in the same region.

➤ Volume discounts: Your sales team may be incentivizing the customer by giving them volume discounts.

Potential solution

Accept the large orders but deliver in multiple shipments to avoid the large spike in demand created by one large shipment.

➤ Minimum order quantities: Your manufacturing operations have large setup costs to switch from one product to another. Manufacturing managers will want large batch sizes to reduce costs. In this case, an organization creates demand variation internally, rather than externally, created by the customer.

Potential solution

Adopt Lean practices on the manufacturing floor to reduce changeover time between production runs so smaller batches become economical.

> Promotions: Many organizations shoot themselves in the foot by creating additional volatility with incentive programs driven by management. Their demand-generation activities create a spike in demand.

Potential solution

Educate management on the additional cost created by these demand spikes. Then, they can weigh this information with the perceived revenue increases resulting from these promotional campaigns. I say "perceived" because promotions could be merely changing the timing of demand, with no net increase.

Anything that reduces this artificial volatility will translate into improved forecast accuracy and better supply chain performance. Rather than passively accepting the status quo, we are acting proactively. We are shaping demand.

Demand Shaping

According to pop culture blogger Peter Jensen Brown, the term "happy hour" as it relates to entertainment and relaxation originated in the US Navy over one hundred years ago.[5] Sailors would watch movies, play music, or even box and wrestle in early evening parties. They had cigars, ice cream, and alcohol in these "happy hours" events.

Then, in the 1920s, during prohibition, it became popular to descend to underground speakeasies to have a few illegal

---

5 Peter Jensen Brown, "History and Etymology of 'Happy Hour,'" Early Sports and Pop Culture History Blog, (2014).

cocktails. Because restaurants were booze-free, these bars became busy in the early evenings before dinner. These illegal sessions also started to become known as happy hours. After the abolishment of Prohibition in 1933, the happy hour idea stuck. However, it was not until the 1970s that bars started offering discounted drinks and food to help fill the bars during otherwise slow times, around 5 p.m. to 7 p.m.

You might be asking what this has to do with demand shaping. Well, happy hours are a form of demand shaping. In other words, in situations with capacity constraints, we can maximize revenue by offering incentives during off-peak hours. Similarly, airlines and hotels use these techniques to adjust prices to encourage travelers to travel during less popular periods.

In this case, the motivation to shape demand is to reduce volatility and so improve forecastability.

Once we have identified the practices that cause artificial volatility, the goal is to reengineer these practices to smooth these demand patterns. This results in better customer service, lower inventory, and reduced costs with no additional investment in technology or people.

Chapter Summary

- ➤ **Be wary of human intervention**. It often renders the forecast less accurate. Avoid seeing patterns that do not exist.

- ➤ **Forecast value add (FVA)** measures the accuracy of the published forecast versus the naive forecast. If you find that the naive version is better, then it is time to reengineer the forecast process.

➤ Differentiate **inherent versus artificial demand volatility**. Investigate the underlying reasons for artificial volatility and minimize them whenever possible.

➤ **Shape demand** to reduce artificial volatility. In situations with capacity constraints, develop strategies to move demand from periods of overload to slow periods.

Chapter 6

Which Items to Forecast

Simplicity is the ultimate sophistication.

—Clare Boothe Luce, US ambassador, author, and politician

Many of you will have heard the story of when enemy soldiers called a temporary amnesty on Christmas Day during World War I and played an impromptu football match on the battlefield. In this chapter, I will share a story about when I created a temporary amnesty with the sales team by radically reducing the number of items to forecast. I was immensely popular for some time with the sales team. The effect was not as dramatic as the Christmas Day amnesty, but the typical tensions with the sales organizations thawed for a while. We all knew that restoration of the natural equilibrium would happen soon, and we would (figuratively) start firing bullets at each other again. But it was nice while it lasted.

When Less Is More

From my experience, most organizations can radically cut the number of forecasted items. I know it sounds counterintuitive, but by focusing your attention on items that must truly be forecasted, the accuracy of the remaining items will increase.

It is an example of when less is more. The concept is similar to the benefits of the Agile approach to software development.

Before Agile came along, software development was quite dysfunctional. In a nutshell, the old approach was that users would ask for everything but the kitchen sink in the software. Developers would then sit behind a curtain for months on end until finally, they resurfaced to reveal their beautiful newborn baby. **They would throw it over the wall to the users**, wash their hands, and celebrate another success.

Meanwhile, the users on the other side of the wall would shake their collective heads. Instead of a beautiful baby, they saw a baby so ugly that they could not even look at it. The software fell extremely short of everyone's expectations and was completely unusable. Agile minimizes these issues with several key strategies, the most critical of which is the concept of the minimum viable product (MVP).

The team asks, "What is the MVP, or what are the minimum requirements to make the software viable?" As you might expect, users spend about eighty percent of their time on twenty percent of the software functionality, so get those working first, and worry about the less popular functions later. For example, I have been a user of Microsoft Excel for many, many years, but I have barely scratched the surface when it comes to using all its functionality. Has anyone ever used the BESSELI function? Me neither! It returns the modified Bessel function of the first kind.[6] There, you cannot claim that you have not learned something valuable from this book.

The same concept applies to forecasting. First identify the minimum viable forecast (MVF). In other words, **which items must we truly forecast?**

---

6   "BESSELI function," Microsoft Support, n.d.

Now with less time wasted on unnecessary items, the focus on the critical ones will yield better results. Why? Forecasting is very much about data analysis. More time spent on analyzing demand data will translate into better and deeper insights, and consequently, reduced forecast error.

Now that we understand the benefits, it is time to look at the specific strategies that will support the ability to prune forecasted items.

Convert Independent to Dependent Demand

For all those bakers out there, how many eggs do you need to make a cake? Obviously, that will **depend** upon the cake. In other words, the demand for a cake ingredient is **dependent** upon the recipe for the cake that we are baking. The egg has dependent demand, and the cake has independent demand.

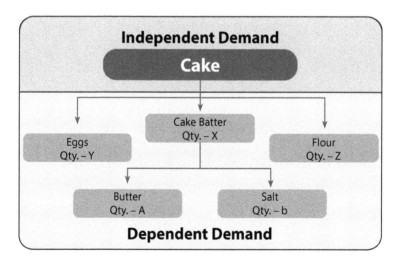

Figure 11: Illustration of independent vs. dependent demand.

The principle here is that we must only forecast items with **independent demand,** and there is no need to forecast those with **dependent demand.** In sales forecasting, it is not the baker making these demand decisions, it is the customer. And it is not the recipe that determines dependent demand, but the BOM.

But what if we could convert the independent demand to dependent demand so they no longer require a forecast? This is not as good as turning water into wine, but it will make you popular with the sales guys! I found from experience that it is indeed possible.

Here is an example: My first professional job was at a manufacturing site that produced consumables for medical devices, and it was part of my job to forecast them. At least, that was the assumption. These consumable items checked all the boxes for independent demand. Customers purchased them, and they had a BOM. You know what they say—if it walks like a duck, swims like a duck, and quacks like a duck, then it is probably a duck. So, I took the tried and trusted approach of forecasting these consumable items. But, one day it occurred to me that the consumable demand is related to the number of instruments actively used by customers. I asked, "Why don't we just forecast the active instruments?"

Based upon historical demand, we could then calculate the relationship between instruments and consumables, which is not going to change dramatically from month to month. One instrument could have ten to twenty different consumables, so now we must only create one forecast. Not Nobel Prize material, but quite revolutionary for demand management at that organization.

Now, we just needed to define the relationship between active instrument demand and consumables. That is when I discovered forecast planning bills of material.

Forecast Planning Bill of Material (FPBOM)

A forecast planning bill of materials (FPBOM) is a special type of BOM. An FPBOM structures the relationship between the instrument and consumable demand. Unlike typical BOMs, we use FPBOMs for forecasting purposes, rather than actual production.

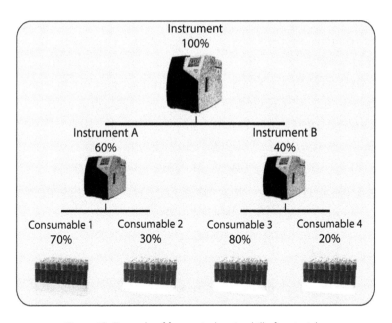

Figure 12: Example of forecast planning bill of materials.

With the help of the sales team, I developed an FPBOM that represented the consumable demand per month per active instrument at a customer site. Then we forecasted the active instruments, and the FPBOM took care of the consumable demand. Every three to six months, we adjusted the FPBOM based upon recent data. Awesome, right? Well, I thought it was exciting, anyway.

SPARE PARTS

Another notable example of demand type conversion is the demand for spare parts, otherwise known as repair parts or service parts. As the name suggests, the field team uses these parts to fix equipment, devices, etc. These spare parts fulfill two distinct types of need:

Preventative maintenance (PM): Field service inspects expensive equipment on a periodic basis. They will identify certain items to replace each time. These are known as inspection consumables. For example, when you take your car in for its 30,000-mile maintenance, there are certain items that the mechanics will automatically replace. Typically, these include oil, cab, and air filters; these are the inspection consumables. In this car example, we could develop a model for the relationship between the number of active cars and the inspection consumable requirements. Voila! No spare part forecast required for this demand type.

Unscheduled repairs: The purpose of preventative maintenance is to reduce the number of unscheduled repairs required due to equipment breakdown. Hopefully, by following your car's PM schedule, you can avoid being stuck on the shoulder of a freeway, waiting for the tow truck to arrive. But no matter the number of PMs, these unscheduled repairs will still happen. Therefore, this demand is not dependent on a PM schedule. You may be able to find another factor that these unscheduled repairs are based upon, such as equipment install base and equipment age profile. However, the relationship is more unpredictable and difficult to quantify. In that case, it will be necessary to treat this demand type as independent, and alas, it will require a forecast.

Assemble to Order (ATO)

Here is another example of forecasting wizardry. In this case, I will reduce the number of forecasted items from x *times* y to x *plus* y.

Example

In the pharmaceutical industry, many regulatory bodies in the world have unique packaging requirements. The pills in the bottle are the same, but the packaging will be different. If the pharmaceutical company had ten medications, and there were eighty different packaging requirements, then there are eighty different potential combinations. If the company had a make-to-stock (MTS) strategy, they would stock each combination. That is eighty different items that will require a forecast.

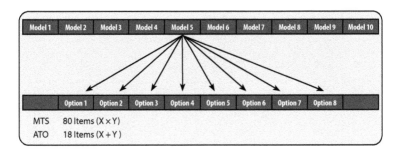

Figure 13: Assemble to order example.

However, instead of stocking every finished goods item based in anticipation of a customer order, what if we changed to an assemble-to-order (ATO) manufacturing strategy? A major advantage of ATO is the radical reduction in forecasted items. In this case, we must still forecast ten medications to know how many unpackaged vials of each medication we require. In addition, we must forecast the eight packaging options to know how many to stock. In other words, we have just reduced the items forecasted from eighty to eighteen !

Pull Versus Push

In this section, we will review the **kanban** approach. This is a technique that, with the right discipline, removes the need for short-term forecasts. Kanban gives replenishment messages when inventory has **actually** reached the reorder point level, not when a forecast **projects** to reach it. In other words, it is a "pull" system, versus the traditional "push" system.

A previously used example was the milk delivery process. When I was a child—in the dark ages—milkmen delivered bottles of milk to houses.

Which Items to Forecast

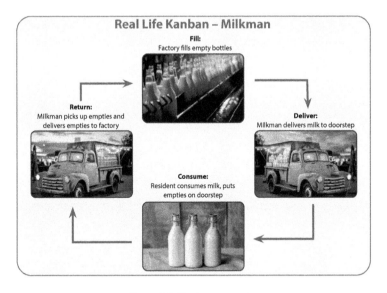

Figure 14: Kanban example.

The process went something like this:

1. Consume: Resident consumes milk, puts empties on doorstep.
2. Return: Milkman picks up empties and delivers empties to factory.
3. Fill: Factory cleans and fills empty bottles.
4. Deliver: Milkman delivers milk to doorstep.

It was quite a slick operation—people placed their "empties" on the front door step each night before they went to bed. When they woke up, the milk fairy had replaced the empties with bottles of fresh milk. We call this a "pull" system because the replenishment signal (empty bottles) is based upon actual consumption, not forecasted consumption.

Why is a pull system more effective for home milk delivery? Well, because daily household demand is not consistent. What if your family goes out of town for a night? In a push system, milk will end up on your doorstep whether or not you need it. For a product with a short shelf life, this could cause lots of unnecessary spoilage. However, in a pull system, if people do not leave empties outside, the milk fairy will fly past your house that morning.

The enormous difference is the control on the amount of inventory in the system. **In a pull system, your inventory cannot exceed the number of kanbans (bottles),** whereas in a push system, there is no limit! I have seen organizations with a year's worth of inventory for an item with a one-week lead time.

Another benefit is that a pull system is self-sustaining and requires minimal daily management. A typical push planning approach requires lots of data input. You need to track your inventory level, open purchase orders, forecast, etc. If this data is inaccurate, you can get a premature replenishment signal (false positive) or you do not receive a signal when needed (false negative). On the other hand, since kanban relies upon visual signals, there is no need for daily data maintenance.

For example, I helped transition a client from MRP to kanban. This client was a manufacturer of expensive electronic instruments. These instruments had over six-hundred items in the BOM, and if one was unavailable, the client shut down the production line. These instruments were extremely expensive, and so a shutdown had an immediate revenue impact. Suffice to say, the project had lots of visibility. Fortunately, the transition to a pull system had the desired impact. Indeed, we reduced production shortages by thirty-seven percent and inventory by thirty percent within twelve months.

In a different example, we implemented kanban for finished goods items at a large medical device manufacturer. The production site assembled these finished goods, which they stored refrigerated in a local warehouse. Unfortunately, the refrigerator was at full capacity. Knowing this, and not seeing any other choice, management had budgeted for a much larger two million dollar refrigerator. However, we implemented kanban with nothing more than a whiteboard, sticky dots, and magnets. After a few weeks we reduced finished goods inventory by over thirty percent, and we avoided the two million dollar cost! In these situations, there is no need for a short-term forecast, and we can reserve forecasting for longer-term planning.

Aggregation/Disaggregation

Consultants sometimes like to use big words when smaller ones would have worked fine. They hope that the large words will make them sound very smart, so you will want to keep paying them the big bucks. This is a perfect example. When describing the approach to forecasting, we could just ask do you use a top-down or bottom-up approach. But that would be too simple, so instead, the fancy words are aggregation and disaggregation, which mean the same. Whatever you want to call it, this concept can seriously reduce the number of items to forecast, so it is worthwhile to understand how it works.

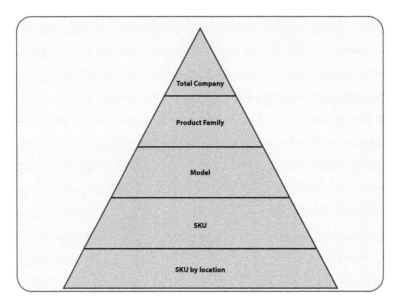

Figure 15: Forecast Hierarchy

The key difference is the starting point for the forecast. In the diagram above, the bottom-up approach requires that we forecast every SKU by location. In this case, to calculate the total forecasts at each level of the hierarchy, the forecasts will be "aggregated." In other words, by summing, or aggregating, the forecasts for all locations, we calculate the global SKU demand. At the base of the hierarchy, the number of items that we must forecast is at its maximum, and so clearly requires the most effort. To lessen the forecasting load, it is possible to aggregate data up to a more forecastable level. Not only are there fewer items to forecast, but the forecasts will be more accurate. Sound too good to be true? It is not, because of what is known as the Law of Large Numbers.

> ## Law of Large Numbers
>
> The concept states that as the sample size grows, its mean will get closer to the mean of the population. For example, we know that if we flip a coin one thousand times, about five hundred of the tosses will be heads, and about five hundred will be tails. In other words, there is a fifty percent chance of either heads or tails. However, what if we reduce the sample size from one thousand to six tosses? How confident are you that the result will be exactly three heads and three tails? I can tell you that I would not place a very high bet on that outcome.
>
> In summary, it makes sense that the results from one thousand tosses will be closer to 50/50 (the population mean) than the results from six tosses.

By aggregating the forecast data, we are creating a larger sample size, which will mean that the results are easier to predict. However, there comes a point of diminishing returns. At a certain point, the aggregation starts to mask important patterns.

For example, if you are forecasting global summer dress demand, you would expect to have reverse seasonality in the northern and southern hemispheres. If you aggregated global historical sales data, you would completely miss this seasonality when disaggregating. In other words, you had forecasted too many sales in the northern hemisphere during its winter and vice versa.

In this case, the forecast should not aggregate to the global level. Since the optimal level is somewhere between the top and bottom levels, we refer to the resulting forecast as "middle-out" forecasting. In this middle-out approach, we forecast at an intermediate level and then sum up to higher levels. Then that forecast is allocated down to the lower levels where data is noisier and less predictable.

Chapter Summary

➤ Forecast only the items that have **independent demand**. Seek opportunities to treat some finished goods items, such as consumables, as dependent demand to create the minimum viable forecast (MVF).

➤ A **forecast planning bill of material (FPBOM)** defines the relationship between the independent demand items and the finished goods with dependent demand.

➤ An **assemble-to-order (ATO)** manufacturing strategy can dramatically reduce the number of items we must forecast, versus a make-to-stock (MTS) strategy. With an MTS strategy, we must forecast all model and option combinations, whereas with an ATO strategy, we can forecast models and options separately. In other words, from an algebraic perspective, the number of forecasted items changes from $x * y$ to $x + y$, where x is the number of models, and y is the number of options.

➤ A **"pull" system** only triggers replenishment when inventory actually falls to the reorder point level. In a "push" system, replenishment is based upon projected demand. A pull system, a.k.a. kanban, is self-managing, and, therefore, short-term forecasts are no longer necessary.

> **Forecast hierarchies** allow us to take advantage of the Law of Large Numbers by forecasting fewer items with more accuracy. However, there is a point at which aggregation masks important patterns.

Chapter 7

Focus on Less!

It is not always that we need to do more but rather we need to focus on less.

—Nathan W. Morris, American writer.

What do the following have in common: software bugs, workplace hazards, health care costs, wealth, customer complaints, and item demand? It is difficult to see how anything could tie these things together. But there is one—the **Pareto principle**, otherwise known as the **80/20 rule**. In general, the principle states that 20 percent of inputs account for 80 percent of outputs. This 80/20 ratio is not exact, but it is remarkable how often the ratio is close. The table below shows specific examples:

Subject	80/20 relationship
Software bugs	20% of software bugs cause 80% of software crashes
Workplace hazards	20% of hazards account for 80% of injuries
Healthcare costs	20% of patients incur 80% of healthcare cost
Wealth	20% of the population holds 80% of financial wealth
Item demand	20% of items account for 80% of revenue

Table 1: Examples of the Pareto principle.

Knowledge of this principle can be very advantageous. For example, knowing that 20 percent of workplace hazards account for 80 percent of injuries means we can focus our resources on creating a safer workspace. For the purposes of this chapter, the last item on the table is interesting. It tells us that a small proportion of the items account for the majority of the revenue. In other words, not all items are equal and deserve different amounts of our attention.

ABC Item Stratification

The Pareto principle is the basis for the ability to perform ABC stratification. Here, the "A" items are the 20 percent that account for 80 percent of usage. On the other end of the spectrum, half of items account for a mere 5 percent of usage. These are the "C" items. In the middle there are the "B" items, which are 30 percent of the total item count and 15 percent of usage.

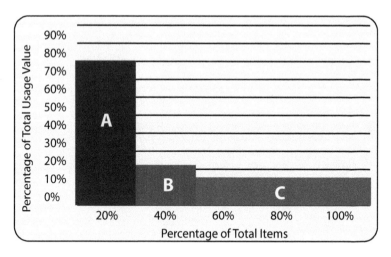

Figure 16: Example of ABC stratification.

How does this knowledge help? Just like the 80/20 rule helps us know which safety risks to focus on, we can leverage it to know which items we should focus our attention on. A items are only

20 percent of total items, but they require 80 percent of demand planning effort, commensurate with their usage value.

On the other end of the spectrum are the C items. Since the C items are about 50 percent of total, but only 5 percent of usage value, then you will want to find ways to radically reduce the time spent on these items.

One effective approach is for us to consolidate the number of locations where we store C items. In other words, if your organization has several distribution centers (DCs), it is worth considering centralizing the storage of these items into one selected DC. Since these items account for half of the total, this could be a substantial reduction in forecasted items. As we will learn later, smaller demand equates to more forecast error. Therefore, by centralizing distribution we can not only reduce forecasted items, but make them more accurate, too.

Now that we are focused on the right items, the next question is how far into the future should we forecast these items?

Detailed Forecast Time Fence

As we learned in the last chapter, there is typically a forecast hierarchy. It can include multiple levels, but for the purposes of this example, we will assume a quite simple pyramid:

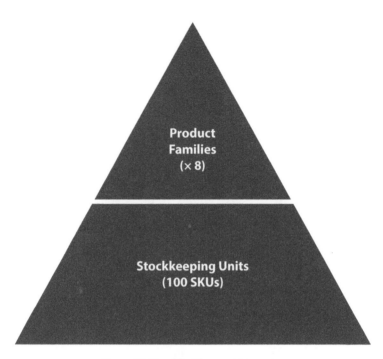

Figure 17: Simplified forecast hierarchy.

In the example above, you can see that there are one-hundred SKUs and only eight product families. I don't know about you, but I prefer not to forecast one-hundred SKUs unless absolutely necessary—eight product families sound much more civilized.

The key question, therefore, is how long do we require a forecast at the SKU level before we can transition to the product family level?

To answer this question, we should remind ourselves why we require a forecast. In the short term, a detailed SKU-level forecast drives demand for production and material plans. For example, it informs buyers which materials to purchase and when. In the case below, the cumulative lead time is seventeen weeks, including procurement and manufacturing—this is how far we require a detailed forecast.

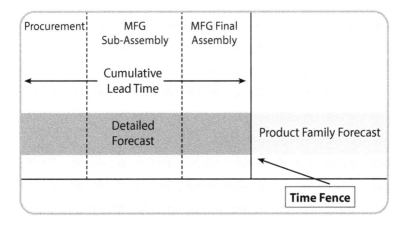

Figure 18: Example of forecast time fence.

We only require a product family forecast after seventeen weeks! This forecast does not drive material requirements but helps calculate capacity requirements for critical resources. I will explain how this process works in a later chapter.

Many organizations will insist upon a detailed forecast for twelve to eighteen months, but why? At one of my clients, they asked the sales team to forecast at the detailed level for five years. No, I'm not joking! Their rationale was that they were heavily regulated, and it could take several years to obtain approval for additional manufacturing sites. But that is not a solid argument. As we just learned, a forecast at the product family level will be enough to project capacity requirements.

Chapter Summary

➤ **Pareto principle (80/20 rule)** states that 20 percent of inputs create 80 percent of outputs. One application of this rule is item ABC stratification. Since A items account for 80 percent of usage value, then that is where to focus your attention, even though they are only 20 percent of total items.

➤ **C items** account for 50 percent of total items, but only 5 percent of usage value. We should spend as little time as possible on these items.

➤ A **detailed forecast** is necessary for as long as the cumulative lead time of raw material procurement and manufacturing. After this detailed forecast time fence, forecasts can be at the product family level.

Chapter 8

Select the Right Forecast Strategy

Make sure that you always have the right tools for the job. It is no use trying to eat a steak with a teaspoon and a straw.

—Anthony T. Hincks, author

I f we must forecast items, then we might as well use the best tool available. How do we figure out what the best tool is? The answer lies in two critical bits of information about the item's demand: demand volatility and demand volume.

Demand Volatility

As discussed earlier, more demand volatility translates to less accurate forecasts. For example, I grew up in Northern England and moved to California in my mid-twenties. For my first few years in California, I lived in the San Joaquin Valley (SJV). Immediately after I arrived, I noticed that the weather was very stable compared to England. I often thought about how different it must be for meteorologists in both places, especially during the summer. I would much rather predict the weather in the SJV than back in England.

In the summer, it was pretty certain that it would be sunny, and the temperature would either be hot or ridiculously hot. In England, this could not be further from the truth, especially in my hometown of Manchester, which had more than its fair share of rain. The joke was that we only knew it was summer when the rain got warmer. Those of you who have spent much time in England will know the weather can change in the blink of an eye. I've been to many barbeque parties that have ended up in the garage, as the rain pours outside. A sunny start to the day lures the optimists to invite their friends over to their house, only for conditions to worsen as soon as they send out the invites.

Demand Volume

In addition to demand variability, demand volume is also a major factor in deciding the best forecasting method. Obviously, higher demand volume means higher impact and more attention required, especially if the item has volatile demand, too. In fact, we should apply about eighty percent of resources to these high-demand items, regardless of demand volatility.

Now that we are clear about these principles, we can review the different forecast strategies based upon their volatility and demand:

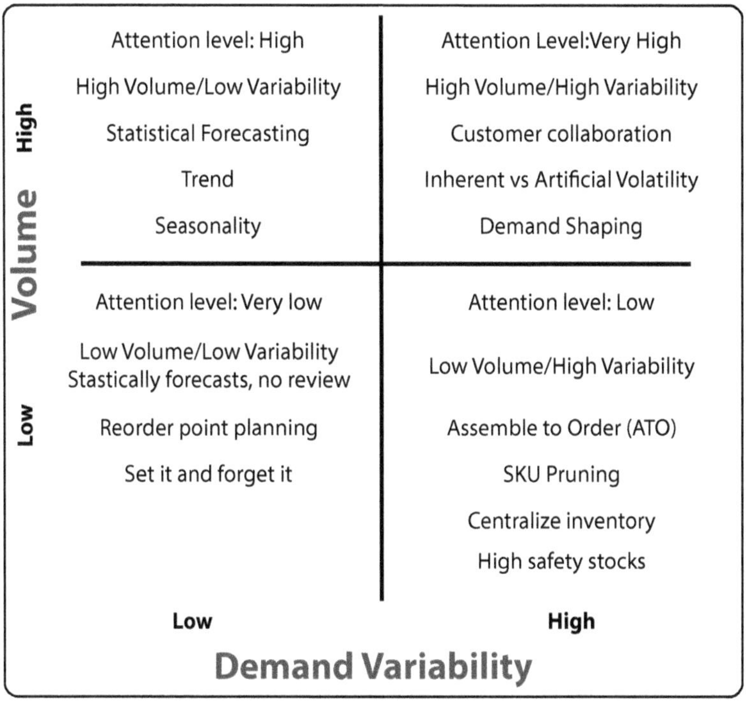

Select the Right Forecast Strategy

	Demand Variability	
Volume High	Attention level: High High Volume/Low Variability Statistical Forecasting Trend Seasonality	Attention Level:Very High High Volume/High Variability Customer collaboration Inherent vs Artificial Volatility Demand Shaping
Volume Low	Attention level: Very low Low Volume/Low Variability Stastically forecasts, no review Reorder point planning Set it and forget it	Attention level: Low Low Volume/High Variability Assemble to Order (ATO) SKU Pruning Centralize inventory High safety stocks
	Low	**High**

Demand Variability

Figure 19: Forecast strategies by volume and demand variability.

Let's look at each quadrant and the strategies best employed for each one.

High Variance, High Volume

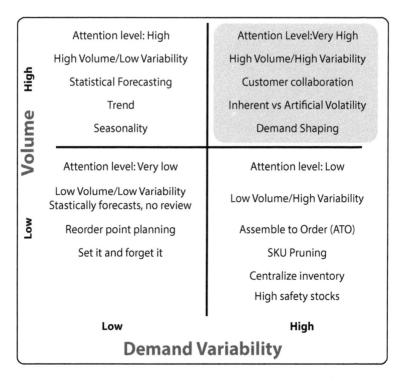

Figure 20: High volume/high demand variability.

These are the items that will cause the most sleepless nights since they have both high volume and high volatility. As discussed earlier, with the Law of Large Numbers, we expect higher demand to result in lower variability. The fact that an item has both high demand and high variability is an anomaly. As explained in Chapter 3, there are two distinct types of volatility—inherent and artificial. You would expect these items to have high artificial volatility, which is the reason for the anomaly.

In my experience, most organizations want to mitigate the risk caused by high volatility with larger safety stock. These are your key items, so you certainly do not want to stockout, right? Unfortunately, this is a futile approach. It will always be difficult to keep enough safety stock. How much is enough, anyway? Those darn customers never run out of ways to surprise you.

Basically, adding safety stock is like placing sandbags around your house in preparation for a major rainstorm. It could work, but if the storm is too heavy, it will overwhelm the sandbags. Safety stock might be sufficient, but if demand exceeds the safety stock, it will not be enough. And the larger the item demand and variability, the bigger the potential tidal wave. As discussed in Chapter 4, the best strategy is not to purchase more sandbags, but to identify and reduce artificial volatility to reduce these tidal waves to a mere ripple.

High Demand, Low Variation

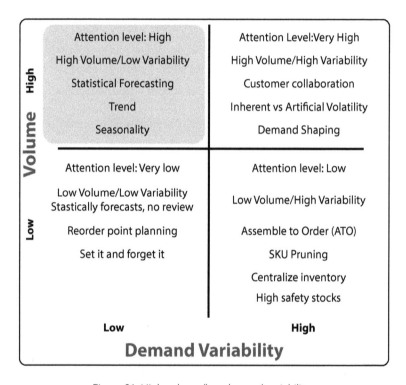

Figure 21: High volume/low demand variability.

For this quadrant, there is one predominant strategy that makes sense—statistical forecasting! Do not worry, I'm not going to go into detailed statistical calculations in this book. It is useful to know, however, that there are multiple techniques ranging from simple to complex algorithms. While it might be tempting to leverage the full array of techniques, just a word of caution. There is a danger if the user does not understand how the software calculated the forecast. **It is never good practice to allow the software to "own" the forecast.**

A person must own the forecast and be able to defend the technique selected. In other words, the system-generated forecast is an input, not necessarily the final output. It is the demand planner and the demand review team who must sanction the final forecast.

A good practice is to start with some of the simpler, easier to understand techniques. For example, the **moving average technique** calculates the average demand over a specified number of recent months (x):

Simple Moving Average Formula

$$\text{"Apr"} = \frac{\text{"Mar"} + \text{"Feb"} + \text{"Jan"}}{3}$$

$$F_t = \frac{A_{t-1} + A_{t-2} + A_{t-3}}{3}$$

"F" = Forecast Demand • "A" = Actual Demand

Figure 22: Example of moving average formula.

A three-month rolling average forecast calculates the average demand over that time period. How to decide how many months to use this method? It is a balancing act. The shorter the time period, the more reactive the forecast will be. This can be helpful if demand is trending up or down, so that your forecast captures this trend. However, the downside is that a shorter range may be over-reactive to random variation. For example, in the most extreme example, a one-month rolling average will be highly reactive, so it is a better practice to measure demand over a longer period. Again, returning to the Law of Large Numbers (LLN), as the number of periods increases, the average demand during that period will tend to move closer to the mean of the population. However, that does not mean that a larger time period is always better. Unlike the toss of a coin, where the probability of landing on heads will always be fifty percent, product demand will shift over time. Demand could be trending up or down, so if you were to use, say, a twelve-month rolling average, your forecast would be terribly slow to react to these trends.

In other words, a smaller number of periods works best for items with demand that is trending up or down significantly. Conversely, a greater number of periods works better for products with stable demand.

SEASONALITY

Seasonality makes forecasting a little more complicated. For example, say that you are forecasting ice cream sales. What would happen if summer had just ended, and you used summer sales to forecast demand in the fall and winter? Exactly—you would need to scrap lots of cream.

In the table below, you can see how we calculate seasonality using historical data. We begin by calculating the average monthly sales, which is 98 per month. To quantify the seasonality index for each month we divide each month's average by the total monthly average. For example, July's average sales are 158 units, meaning that it is significantly busier than the average month (98 units), and its seasonality index will be greater than 1.0. As you can see in the table, July's seasonality index is 1.62. December has the lowest seasonality at 0.42.

Select the Right Forecast Strategy

Month	3 Year Data				Monthly Avarage	Seasonal Index
	2015	2016	2017	3 Yr Avg		
Jan	55	56	54	55	98	0.57
Feb	62	65	68	65	98	0.66
Mar	85	97	88	90	98	0.92
Apr	98	99	110	102	98	1.05
May	130	127	141	133	98	1.35
Jun	150	140	157	149	98	1.52
Jul	165	152	158	158	98	1.62
Aug	155	138	153	149	98	1.52
Sep	92	94	99	95	98	0.97
Oct	72	75	74	74	98	0.75
Nov	61	66	64	64	98	0.65
Dec	41	44	38	41	98	0.42
Total	1166	1153	1204	1175	1175	1.00

Table 2: Seasonality Index calculation.

Low Demand, High Variation

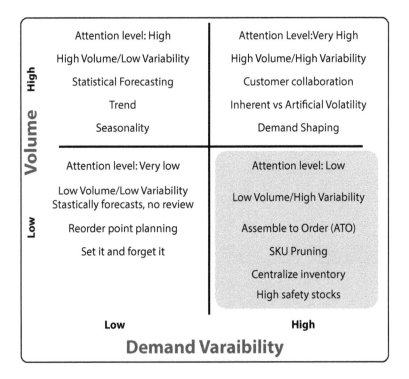

Figure 23: Low volume/High demand variability.

These items are the worst because sales volume is low, but demand variability is high, meaning they require some attention. However, there are several strategies that can reduce the amount of attention required:

SKU Pruning

These items are difficult to forecast and provide little reward for improving forecasting accuracy. In other words, they are annoying! My first response when I see this category is, "Can we get rid of them?" Would it be possible to give the product portfolio a haircut and trim items with low demand? I encourage your organization to consider this option. If it is possible to accurately calculate the true profitability of items in this category, you might get a nasty surprise. On the surface, they may seem profitable, but under the surface, there are additional costs lurking, such as slow inventory turns, high scrap rates, increased expedited costs, etc.

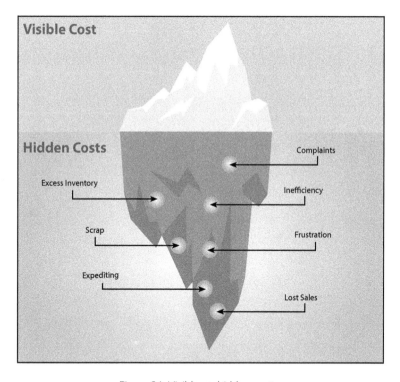

Figure 24: Visible vs. hidden costs.

Unfortunately, many organizations are loath to discontinue any SKUs that contribute even a minimal amount to sales revenue.

But, if you can calculate the total cost, then you are more likely to get executive attention. Assuming there are still some of these low volume, elevated risk items remaining, there are several other strategies that will help the forecasting effort.

Assemble-to-Order (ATO)/Make-to-Order (MTO)

As discussed earlier in the book, ATO/MTO strategies can help reduce forecasting requirements. This is especially true when demand variation is high, and volumes are low.

For example, imagine that you and your significant other go to your favorite Italian restaurant. You are celebrating your anniversary, which is why you have decided to splash out. As always, your partner orders the same dish—ribeye, medium rare. She always asks to substitute the mashed potatoes for rice and asks your server to put the dressing on the side. In this type of restaurant, you expect that the server will grant these requests. This is analogous to our low demand, high variation situation.

Most orders will have some change requested, so it would be an expensive mistake to try to forecast every scenario and prepare these meals ahead of time—a make-to-stock (MTS) strategy. You can imagine the amount of food that the restaurant would scrap at the end of every day. But this is not what happens. In this environment, a restaurant will only prepare your dish after they have taken your order, so it does not need to forecast every option—MTO or ATO strategy. On the other hand, fast food restaurants have a MTS inventory strategy. Hence the word "fast." Their goal is to stock everything on the menu, so the customer's wait time is minimal.

Centralize Inventory

Another strategy is to centralize inventory. We discussed this topic earlier when we reviewed best practices for managing C items. This strategy calls for centralizing the inventory deployment of these items. Consolidation of inventory into fewer distribution centers will reduce demand volatility and increase forecast accuracy.

Higher safety stocks

This strategy is often the first resort for many organizations. For me, though, it is the last resort. The key difference is that the previous options reduced overall supply chain costs. Safety stock, on the other hand, increases costs by increasing inventory holding costs. If it is a choice between higher costs and excess inventory shortages, then safety stock is typically the better option. Earlier in the book, we reviewed how to optimize safety stocks based upon demand variation, lead time variation, and desired service levels. Again, consider all the other options described above before settling on higher safety stocks.

Low Demand, Low Variation

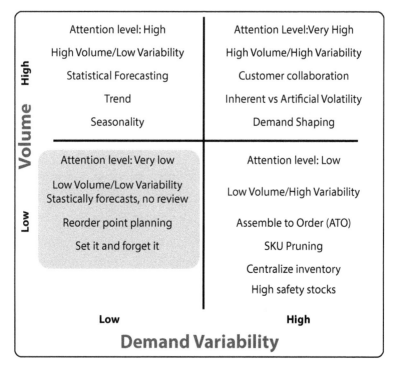

Figure 25: Low volume/low demand variability.

You should not spend time on these low-demand and low-variability items. The term "set it and forget it" applies here. You can statistically forecast these items without any review. Alternatively, to minimize the effort required, put them on a reorder point program. This planning method requires much less data than MRP and is much easier to manage and maintain. All you must know is your current inventory level, supply lead times, safety stock, order quantities, and daily demand estimates to calculate the reorder point. We often refer to this as the Min-Max method.

Reorder point and minimum inventory level (MIN) are synonymous with each other. I will quickly walk you through an example to show how easy it is to calculate:

> Example: Buy Item Number A1234
> Daily demand = 20 units
> Supplier lead time = 10 working days

To begin with, we must calculate the demand during lead time (DDLT). In other words, this is an estimate of how much inventory we will consume from the time we place a purchase order with a supplier to when we expect it to arrive.

DDLT = Lead time (days) x Daily Demand = 10 days x 20 units/day = 200 units

---

This means that if you place an order when inventory is at 200 units, the order should arrive just as your inventory drops to zero. But I think the most important word in the previous sentence is **should.** How much money would you bet on sales being exactly 20 units per day during this period, and that the supplier delivers the order on exactly day 10? I am definitely keeping my hands in my pocket for this one.

As we know, our supply chains often stray from the happy path. We could sell more than 200 units, or the supplier may deliver late. Therefore, it would be wise to add a buffer (safety stock) to the reorder point to guard against these deviations from the plan. There are statistical methods to optimize safety stock, based upon demand variation and desired service levels, but I will not get into that here. For more details on statistical forecast techniques, read

Nicolas Vandeput's *Demand Forecasting Best Practices*, referenced in the "Recommended Reading" section at the end of the book. For now, we will assume that you want to maintain a safety stock of 50 units. In other words, we will increase the reorder point from 200 to 250 units using this formula:

Reorder point (MIN) = Lead time x Daily Demand + Safety Stock

---

Now, this method will trigger a reorder message once the available inventory falls below 250 units.

Great, now we know **when** to place the order, the next question will be **how much?** This will depend upon several factors but consider how often you would like to order this item. For example, what if you decide that you want to place a purchase order once per month? Using the example above again, daily demand was 20 units, so assuming a month has 20 working days, then the order quantity would be around 400 units (20 units x 20 days).

The next step is to calculate the MAX inventory level. This is the maximum inventory that you want on hand at any time. Theoretically, the MAX inventory level would be your MIN level plus your order quantity.

MAX = MIN + Order Quantity

In other words, say you place an order as inventory drops below the reorder point, and for some reason, customers stop buying the product. When we deliver the purchase order, your inventory level is still at the MIN level and now you have the order quantity on top of that. This is the worst-case scenario in terms of inventory levels. Once the order quantity arrives, since there was no demand, your inventory would be the MIN plus order quantity. This is the theoretical maximum.

Chapter Summary

> The **right forecasting tool** for any item depends upon demand volatility and demand volume.

> **High demand** and **high volatility** items require the most attention. Find out which customer(s) are causing the high variation and explore alternative strategies to level load demand. Better collaboration with these customers to understand demand patterns is advisable in this situation.

> **High demand** and **low variation** items lend themselves nicely to statistical forecasting techniques.

> If **demand seasonality** exists, it is important to factor that into the forecast.

> **Low demand** and **high variation** items are exceedingly difficult to forecast due to the sporadic nature of their demand. Ideally, we will prune these items from the product portfolio. For these items, adopt an MTO or ATO inventory strategy, if possible. These strategies will reduce the items that we must forecast.

> **Low demand** and **low variation** items should receive little attention from us. My suggestion is to calculate MIN and MAX levels and put them on a reorder point program.

Chapter 9

Executing the Forecast Strategy

Ideas are easy; it's the execution that separates the sheep from the goats.

—Sue Grafton, American author.

I grew up in England in the 1980s, when unemployment rates reached twelve percent. My dad was one of the unfortunate ones who lost their jobs. To make ends meet, he did all sorts of odd jobs, one of which was gardening. At the time, I was a teenager, and I would often help him out to earn some extra cash. One Saturday morning, we went to one of his regulars to work on their front yard. A few days earlier, a friend had given my dad an electric lawnmower. Since he already had one, he was hoping to sell it to the customer we were working for that day. He set up a demonstration in the front yard, and before long, he had closed the sale. We agreed to use it to finish the front lawn. My dad had a few things to discuss with her in the backyard, so he handed the lawnmower over to me and left me to it.

He had made it look amazingly easy to use, but I soon found out that it was not as simple as it seemed. The primary difficulty was that the ground was quite uneven and worse, the dirt was dry. I found myself needing to apply some effort to get the blades over some of the large lumps. When the lawnmower protested,

I pushed even harder. I was so focused on getting the better of the lawn, I had not noticed a steady plume of black smoke coming from the motor. Meanwhile, as my dad was chatting to the nice old lady at the back of the house, he started to notice this dark smoke rising over the roof. It took a few minutes for him to realize where the smoke was coming from, but by then it was too late. I had well and truly burned out the motor, and my dad was understandably upset. Furious would be a more accurate description. Needless to say, he lost out on some much-needed money, and he did not trust me with any electrical gardening equipment for a long time afterward.

My reason for recounting this story is to illustrate that the correct tool and proper execution are of equal importance.

In the last chapter, I explained how to select the correct tool. In this chapter, we will drill down into some details on how to effectively use these tools and avoid the black smoke.

Market Intelligence

The COVID-19 pandemic seared an especially important lesson into the heads of supply chain professionals everywhere—namely, you cannot rely upon historical demand to calculate forecasts. As we know, the demand for items like toilet paper in the weeks after the pandemic had extraordinarily little resemblance to the pre-pandemic demand. This happened to many products where demand exceeded expectations or fell off a cliff. Pandemics do not happen every day, but lesser examples do happen frequently, with potentially severe repercussions. For example, in Chapter

3, I described how failure to communicate a three-fold demand increase caused many sleepless nights.

This is where your sales team can add the most value. Their value is not so much using historical demand data to create forecasts. You do not need to be a salesperson to operate a spreadsheet. In fact, I know a few salespeople who would prefer to stick needles in their eyes than spend much time using formulas to calculate forecasts. This is not a problem, since we want salespeople to focus on growing revenue.

To make everyone's life easier and to reduce friction, I recommend that since the supply chain team is more motivated to develop an accurate forecast, give that responsibility to the them. Once you have developed the statistical forecast, share the key items with the sales team. They can then add any market intelligence that would not be captured by historical data.

In my experience, this gets the best of both worlds: a more accurate forecast with enough market intelligence built in, while allowing the sales team to focus their time on selling more products.

Opportunities/Risks

Whenever the sales team provides market intelligence, there is always a dilemma about whether to include or exclude the impact of uncertain events. For example, perhaps they have become aware of a potential large project that could drive demand much higher than the current forecast. Should we include this information or not? In these situations, the salesperson must weigh up the probabilities and decide. If we exclude the information, but it happens, then we consider this as an opportunity. Conversely, if we include the information in the forecast, it is a risk, since it may not happen.

> **OPPORTUNITIES are events that MAY happen but are EXCLUDED from the forecast.**
> **RISKS are events that MAY NOT happen but are INCLUDED in the forecast.**

If you want to get more sophisticated, we could include a percentage probability and apply it to all significant market intelligence. So what? How does this help the supply chain team?

Opportunity/Risk

Opportunities/ Risks	Quantity	Actions	Responsiblity	Due Date

Table 3: Opportunity/Risk Tracking.

In the case of opportunities, it may be worthwhile to front-load the production plan, so if the opportunity occurs, then capacity is available for the increase. In addition, it could be worthwhile to temporarily increase safety stock of raw materials with long lead times to cover the opportunity. In the case of risks, it is possible to delay making commitments to suppliers until more information becomes available. In either case, the more agility built into the supply chain, the more capable you are of reacting quickly to these changes before they create expensive problems.

Collaboration

Collaboration with key customers can also be instrumental in reducing forecast errors. This requires much more work than statistical forecasting, and there is no guarantee that the customer will have any special insights into future demand. But, if only one customer purchases the product, or their demand accounts for a large slice of the total, then open up these communication channels. Customer input should yield better forecast accuracy overall.

For example, at a pharmaceutical manufacturing client, there was one product in particular that only had one customer, and its revenue was significant. At first, there was minimal collaboration with this customer, and their orders were always a challenge to predict. Since it was an MTS item with a shelf life, it was either feast or famine. When they exceeded projected demand, they often encountered delays. Conversely, lighter than expected demand could result in expired materials. Nobody was satisfied with the status quo. However, once we initiated better communication with the customer, life became much better for everyone involved. It turned out that the customer in question was a government entity. As is the case with many of these public institutions, much bureaucracy existed, and it could take them many weeks to approve their order. We asked that the salesperson receive notification from the customer at the start, not the end of the approval process. Since the customer always approved these requests, my client could now use the earlier notification as the trigger for final assembly. Once the customer finally placed the order, the product was sitting on the shelf and ready to go. Everyone was happy!

Forecast Unit of Measure

In the calendar year 2022, the US Department of Treasury, Bureau of Engraving and Printing (BEF) produced **six billion notes** worth an estimated $267.1 billion, in the following denominations:

Denomation	2022 orders (billions)	
	Number of notes	% of total
$1	10B	17%
$20	2.5B	42%
$100	2.0B	33%
Other	0.5B	8%
Total	6.0B	100%

Table 4: US Treasury Department currency note production, 2022-2023.

I selected this anecdote to present the one case of when it is acceptable to use US dollars as the only forecast unit of measure. The Treasury has a pass; nobody else does!

Unbelievably, I have experienced situations where the sales team believes that they only need to provide a quarterly forecast in US dollars. Thanks, guys! To reiterate, we must receive the forecast in units, unless you work for the Treasury. By all means, forecast revenue, too, but do not forget the item count, please!

Executing the Forecast Strategy

Volume Versus Mix

Staying with the treasury, how do we calculate the mix of notes that we must produce? For example, in the following year, 2023, the Treasury reduced their order from six to five billion notes. Let's imagine for a minute that this year, the Treasury got lazy and decided not to include the mix of notes required. The production planners would need to figure out which notes to produce. They would analyze the 2022 order, which did provide that level of detail, and calculate 2023 note requirements using the same percentage breakdown.

Here is what would have happened:

Denomation	2022 orders (billions)		2023 orders (billions)	
	Number of notes	% of total	Projection	Actual
$1	10B	17%	0.8B	2.0B
$20	2.5B	42%	2.1B	0.1B
$100	2.0B	33%	1.7B	1.1B
Other	0.5B	8%	0.4B	1.8B
Total	6.0B	100%	5.0B	5.0B

Table 5: US Treasury Department 2022 currency production, by denomination as a percentage of total bills.

As you can see, they would have been very wrong. The Treasury overordered $20 bills in 2022, since they drastically reduced their order from 2.5 to 0.1 billion. On the other hand, $1 bill orders doubled from one to two billion. If we had relied upon the production planners, the US would have been awash with $20 bills and woefully short of $1 bills.

In other words, we should not ask the supply chain team to figure out the forecast mix when it will be much different from recent history. If the mix is typically consistent, then it is not a problem; otherwise, the supply chain team should request the mix detail.

Intervals

Interval is the technical term often referred to as "buckets." Let me ask a simple question. What do we do with a forecast in quarterly or annual buckets? Do we assume that demand is equal in each three-month period as it is throughout the year? This may be accurate, but oftentimes, this would be an inaccurate assumption. Ensure that the forecast is in small enough buckets that you are not left guessing on how to break down the forecast into the necessary level of detail.

ANNUAL FORECASTS

If we receive one annual forecast, do we divide it by twelve to create equal monthly forecasts? What if there is seasonality? For example, I worked for a company that sold its products to a home improvement retail chain. The retailer liked to promote our products on the large summer bank holidays. Indeed, seventy-five percent of our sales to this customer happened in the period between Memorial Day and Labor Day. Obviously, if we assumed level monthly demand, there would be some severe shortages over the summer. Therefore, annual forecasts definitely do not work for products with a seasonal demand, or any time that level monthly demand is not expected.

QUARTERLY FORECASTS

Quarterly forecasts can also pose a dilemma. We could simply divide each quarterly forecast by three so that each month is equal. But I have worked in organizations where that would be a really bad idea. For example, I have had a few clients that sell expensive, capital-intensive products. At the end of each quarter, there will be a demand surge.

Customers become accustomed to the fact that their suppliers have made quarterly sales commitments to Wall Street. They also know that their suppliers will become increasingly generous with pricing at quarter-end. As a result, customers will often wait until the last couple of weeks of the quarter to place their orders, with an expectation of a sizable discount. In this case, an even distribution of a quarterly forecast over each of the three months would result in significant excess inventory until the end of each quarter. And because you are guessing which items will actually sell, there is a risk that your inventory may not match the customers' orders. This can result in expensive expediting, so that we build what we actually require in the last few weeks. Clearly, this is artificial volatility for which the client is responsible, but the whole industry has ingrained these unhealthy habits. Again, forecasts in quarterly buckets provide insufficient detail if level monthly demand is unexpected.

Time Horizon

I frequently experience clients whose forecast time horizon is simply not long enough. For example, one client's sales team updates their forecast annually. In other words, they submit a forecast in December for the next calendar year. I asked for clarification. Does that mean that at the end of November, there is only a forecast available for December, until the sales team distributes next year's forecast? They nodded their heads sheepishly.

This would have worked fine if the supply chain team could wave a magic wand, and suddenly, suppliers delivered materials to the receiving dock. However, I already knew that the lead time for some of their raw materials was six months, and their manufacturing lead time was one month. In other words, since their total supply chain lead time was seven months, they were increasingly in the dark for the second half of the year regarding the materials required to satisfy demand at the start of the following year.

Worse yet, one client creates a forecast for one quarter at a time but does not distribute this forecast until one to two weeks into the quarter. This means at the start of each quarter there is no forecast. I asked how they knew what to manufacture in the first two weeks, and they said it was an educated guess. Once they publish the forecast, they adjust accordingly.

The supply chain team must communicate how far out they need the forecast, for everyone to be successful. A forecast horizon that at least extends beyond the cumulative lead time should be non-negotiable. Ideally it would extend out eighteen months, so that when we create next year's budget, your forecast extends to the end of the year.

Constrained Versus Unconstrained Forecast

At one renewable energy manufacturer, capacity was seriously constrained. They were only able to produce about forty percent of total demand. That was a monumental problem until capacity came on board several months too late. The sales team had become accustomed to reducing the forecast to fit the capacity. That was a mistake! Your forecast should always begin unconstrained. Otherwise, how will operations know the amount of required capacity? It confuses matters because it mixes both demand and supply planning. In other words, the demand plan considers the supply plan. We should perform these steps sequentially, not in parallel. It is the supply chain team that must evaluate all options before they conclude that they cannot meet some customer demand.

The supply planning process will endeavor to find solutions to any potential constraints. These solutions could include overtime, subcontracting, etc. For the supply team, an inability to meet projected demand will be the last resort.

They will not want to be the reason for missed revenue targets. They will see it as a loss, and sometimes this is unavoidable. However, it is important to not "throw in the towel" before the supply team even sees the forecast. The supply plan will highlight constraints and propose options, if possible. Supply Chain will then present them to executive management, especially if the options require a budget revision.

We will measure progress against the final forecast, whether constrained or unconstrained. For example, we should always use the constrained forecast for financial projections.

Multiple Demand Sources

One pitfall to guard against is not including all demand sources in the forecast. For example, the sales team sometimes "forgets" to include non-revenue generating (NRG) demand, such as products required for customer demos or training purposes. This NRG demand becomes a second-class citizen and not given the respect it deserves. We must still manufacture and distribute this demand, right?

Another example is when Research & Development or Engineering requires materials or products for some form of testing or engineering runs. Their demand can sometimes dwarf commercial demand, but still, nobody forecasted it. Under any of these scenarios, the risk is that an incomplete forecast will result in insufficient inventory. Unless you manage inventory allocation, you could end up fulfilling NRG orders at the expense of the ones that actually generate revenue. Needless to say, ensure your organization understands the importance of communicating all significant demand sources.

Chapter Summary

> ➤ The sales team can add the most value to the forecast process by providing **market intelligence** for any expected demand changes due to external factors. This could include new projects, customer loss, promotions, etc.

Executing the Forecast Strategy

➤ **Opportunities** are potential specific upsides to the published forecast. **Threats** are demand that we included in the forecast, but there is a potential that the demand does not happen. In either case, we should document and quantify them as best as possible.

➤ The supply chain team requires **unit forecasts**, not currency forecasts, unless you are printing money. In which case, good luck!

➤ Forecasts should be at a **detailed level** if demand is quite different than in recent history.

➤ **Forecast intervals** should be in buckets no larger than monthly.

➤ Forecasts must cover the necessary **time horizon.**

➤ Forecasts should always be **unconstrained,** to give the supply chain team the opportunity to develop options to avoid unhappy customers.

➤ It is always necessary to consider all significant **demand sources** to ensure the supply chain team has all the facts before developing the supply plan.

Chapter 10

Balancing Forecasted and Actual Demand

The key to keeping your balance is knowing when you've lost it.

—Anonymous

So far, this book has been primarily focused on what *may* happen. It is the best guess on what the future has in store for us. It is time now to move to where the rubber hits the road (i.e., customer orders). The forecast is the plan, and customer orders are the execution of the plan. As customers place orders, they "consume" the forecast so we do not duplicate demand. When we align forecasts and actual orders, this process works like clockwork. Not to say that it does not happen often, but last time it did, dinosaurs were walking the earth.

Suffice to say, we do not live in a perfect world, especially when it comes to forecasting. This chapter will show how to approach these suboptimal situations where the forecast and actual demand are imbalanced. These are situations that occur daily, so it is critical to understand how to manage them effectively.

Demand Control

Demand control is a set of strategies and practices used to manage and regulate customer demand for products. Its goal is to ensure that the supply chain can efficiently meet customer demand while minimizing disruptions, costs, and risks. When performed effectively, it takes chaos out of the near-term planning process and stimulates timely actions. It is best practice to appoint a demand controller who has the responsibility to monitor daily or weekly orders. Whenever orders differ from the near-term plan, the demand controller will engage the appropriate sales leadership. In addition, the order management software can hold orders when they exceed a defined threshold, so they can review them internally before deciding what action to take.

Demand control will enable a quicker proactive response to potential demand/supply imbalances. Studies have shown that this quicker response can result in inventory reductions of as much as twenty-five percent, and revenue grows as backorders decline.[7]

Let's say, for example, a regional distributor placed an exceptionally large, unforecasted order. By the time the supplier noticed, they had already shipped the inventory. Unfortunately, the very next day, another customer placed an order for the same product. To make matters worse, this customer had actually forecasted their order months beforehand, so you can imagine how the customer received the news that the supplier would not fulfill the order. If this had occurred during the recent pandemic, the supplier's response would have been much slower. As we all remember, by the time grocery stores limited the number of scarce products, such as toilet paper, that individual customers could purchase, it was too late. The pipeline for many items was already dry, and consumers waited a long time for many products.

---

7   David Holmes, Todd Ferguson, and Timm Reiher, "Demand Control: An Often Missing Link in a Demand Management Process," Oliver Wight Americas, 2019.

Never was there a more crucial time to have an effective demand control process.

Available to Promise (ATP)

When a customer places an order, they would like to know when they can expect to receive it. That shouldn't be too much to ask for, should it? I can tell you that most of my clients start between forty and sixty percent on time performance against that promise date. Even airlines might be disappointed with that performance level.

Available-to-promise (ATP) is one practice that can improve that performance quickly. It calculates the availability of the item when the customer requests it.

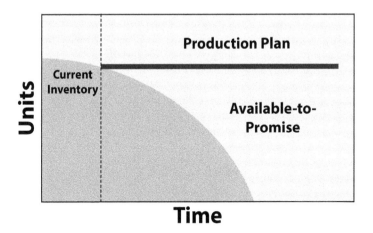

Figure 26: Illustration of available-to-promise.

As you can see from the diagram above, customer orders gradually consume inventory on hand and then the future production plan. If there is insufficient ATP, then the supplier will need policies in place to know what to do next. Sometimes the supplier defines a standard lead time per item, which they can use to calculate when to promise the order.

As with all software functionality, ATP requires accurate data to provide an accurate commitment to the customer. In this case, it requires on-hand inventory, open sales orders, and incoming delivery dates to be accurate.

What I described above assumes that you have an MTS inventory strategy. In other words, the plan is to always keep inventory on the shelf, waiting for customers to place their orders. But what if you have an MTO strategy? In other words, you wait for your customers to order first before you commit to producing more inventory. Obviously, ATP is useless in this environment, as there will never be available inventory to promise. Not to worry, I have one last trick up my sleeve that can address this issue. It is capable-to-promise (CTP).

Capable-to-Promise (CTP)

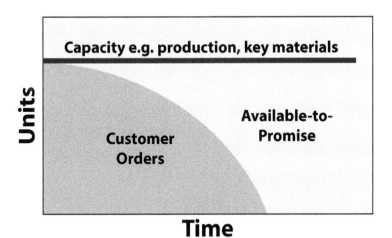

Figure 27: Illustration of capable-to-promise.

In an MTO environment, it is **resources, not finished goods inventory,** that we promise against, and new customer orders consume the resources required to build a product.

Now, this CTP functionality is not for rookies. It requires much more data to calculate availability than ATP. For example, it requires that available capacity be known, which in turn requires accurate item routings, work center data, etc. As they say, "Don't try this at home" unless your organization is committed to managing this data consistently.

Forecast Consumption

Those of you who enjoy literary classics may recognize what George Orwell, Jane Austen, Franz Kafka, Anton Chekhov,

Emily Bronte, and D.H. Lawrence have in common, aside from being renowned writers. They all died from consumption. Two hundred years ago, to receive a diagnosis of consumption—now known as tuberculosis—was a death sentence. Indeed, consumption was a disease which, at its peak, was responsible for twenty-five percent of the deaths in Europe. It starts with a chronic cough, paleness, and a lack of appetite. It then deteriorates quickly, causing wheezing and fever and bringing red blotches to the cheeks. In its final stages, its victim grows emaciated, causing bones to protrude.

That was the scarier type of consumption. On the other hand, forecast consumption, although a little complicated to understand, is not as scary as the other kind.

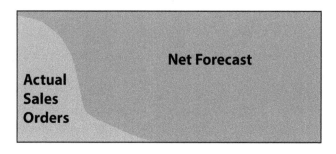

Figure 28: Actual sales orders consuming net forecast.

When a customer places an order, it will consume the forecast, to avoid duplicating demand. But the question is, what rules will we follow to perform this consumption?

Let us start by looking at an example. In the diagram below, you can see that there are four periods, each of which has a forecast, and there are no customer orders yet. The total forecast for these four periods is 2,300 units (600+400+600+700).

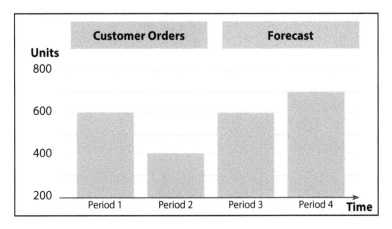

Figure 29: Forecast before customer orders.

Then, the customer places an order for shipment in Period 3 for 1,000 units.

Lean Forecasting Demystified

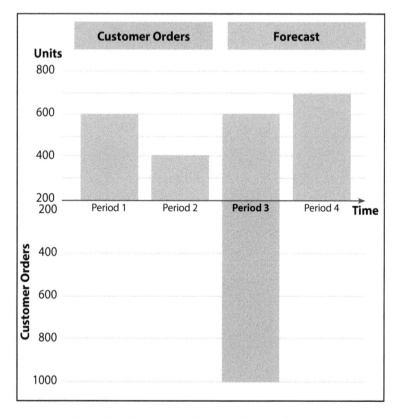

Figure 30: Customer order received against forecast.

Which forecast do we consume? In general, there are three consumption policies:

- ➤ Backward consumption only
- ➤ Forward consumption only
- ➤ Backward/Forward consumption

Most modern enterprise resource planning (ERP) systems allow you to configure any of these policies and the number of consumption periods. In other words, how many periods backward or forward will we need to consume the forecast? In the example below, you can see that consumption is backward and the consumption period is two. The customer order demand consumes all the forecasts in Period 3 and 2.

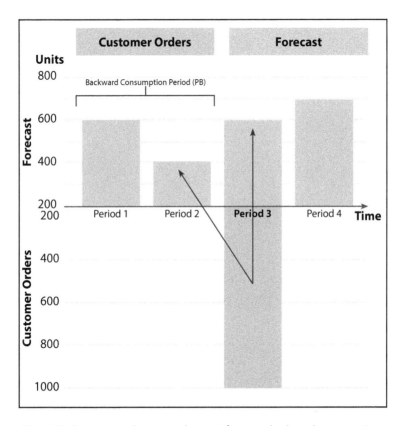

Figure 31: Customer order received against forecast: backward consumption.

If the consumption policy was forward and two consumption periods, then it would look like this:

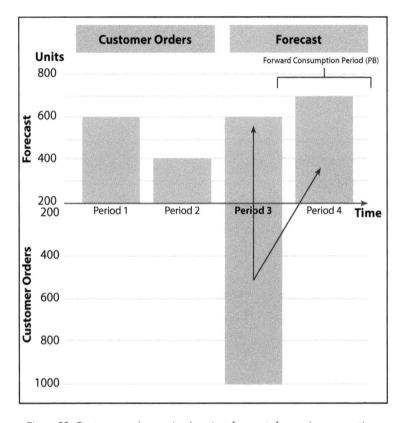

Figure 32: Customer order received against forecast: forward consumption.

Forecast Consumption Policy Selection

Now that you know how each forecast consumption policy works, you want to know why you would pick one policy over another. In general, a larger number of orders for an item will indicate no backward or forward consumption required.

Why? If an item has 1,000 customers that typically place orders each month, an increase or decrease in one month is not likely to impact next month's sales. In other words, because of the substantial number of customers, demand variation is random, and each month's demand is independent of the next. In that case, a large order will consume nothing but the current period.

For example, think about the demand at a local, popular fast-food restaurant. If you had forecasted 1,000 burgers sold each day, and yesterday you sold 1,200 burgers, does that mean you would expect to only sell 800 burgers today? Probably not, because the demand on any given day is independent. In this case, you only want to consume the forecast for that day, and not backward or forward days. If you consumed forward, the unconsumed forecast would become 800, which is not what we expect to happen.

What about the other end of the spectrum? An extreme example would be a product with only one forecasted order per month. Say they typically order 1,000 units per month, and last month, they ordered 2,000 units. You would expect that since they doubled their forecasted demand, this month's demand would be much lower, and they would place no orders. In this case, forward consumption seems logical.

Say they did not place any orders last month, so the unconsumed forecast was still 1,000 units. It would be natural for you to predict much larger demand than normal this month. But, if you do not have backward consumption set up, the forecast for the prior month would have disappeared when it quite possibly should not have.

Customer Order Dates

I would like to finish this chapter with what I have found to be excruciatingly difficult, given how simple it seems. I am referring to dates associated with a customer order, including order receipt date, order entry date, request date, original promise date, revised promise date, ship date, delivery date, etc. I may have been just unfortunate, but in my experience, most companies are not aligned on the definition of each date, and they do not manage them effectively. This is not a trivial matter. Without clarity here, we are unable to confidently answer some of the most basic supply chain-related questions:

➤ What is the lead time from when a customer places an order to when it ships or delivers? Is it competitive?

➤ How well do we meet our customer request dates?

➤ How well do we meet our promises of when the customer will get their product?

➤ If there is a delay, do we revise the date, so the customer now knows when to expect it?

Let's do a deep dive on each of these questions:

What is the lead time from when a customer places an order to when it ships or delivers? Is it competitive?

I was working with a client to improve their on-time shipment performance to customers. The objective was to reduce the shipment of fast-moving items from six business days to within one business day. We executed many initiatives to achieve this target, including an updated inventory strategy, streamlined warehouse picking process, capacity planning, and many more. To measure performance, we compared the sales order **ship date** to the **order entry date.** Finally, after a few months of effort, we reduced the median lead time to one business day. We declared victory and held a celebration!

However, we were surprised that we were still receiving complaints from customers that lead times were still unacceptable.

"Those darn customers; they're never happy," was our general response. But to make sure, we dug deeper into some specific orders and found that their complaints were legitimate. The disconnect was that there were some major delays in the order entry process. So, even though we had accelerated the downstream supply chain, the upstream supply chain had in fact slowed down, but we had no visibility to it.

I tell you this story to make a critical point: To measure lead time accurately, it is critical to capture the time when the clock starts ticking and when it stops.

Everybody intuitively understood this, but it still slipped through the cracks. In terms of when the clock starts, it was a simple correction—they started to record the date that they *received* the order from the customer, not the date that they finally *entered it.*

Obviously, we also must know when the clock stops ticking, too. Is it based upon when we made the product available to the customer, when they picked it up, or when we delivered it? Regardless of which one we measure, your customer base must align with this decision for the lead time metric to be meaningful. If you have agreed terms with your customers that you are responsible for delivery, it is not enough to only capture the time that the order ships. That is like running a race and claiming victory at the end of the third lap, when there is still one more lap to run.

How well do we meet our customer request dates?

This is not a revolutionary idea, right? An organization should know how often it is able to meet its customers' request date. However, in my experience, many organizations do not accurately capture when the customer actually requested the product. For this to work, there must be some business rules relating to the **request date.** For example, if the standard lead time for a product is five days, but the customer requests that the order ships tomorrow, which date should we use for the request date? Regardless of what the right answer is for your company, there should be an answer that is consistent throughout the organization.

How well do we meet our promises of when the customer will get their product?

Regardless of when the customer requested their order, a supplier should respond with a commitment that they will fulfill it. Ideally, you want the commit date to be the same date as the request date. Clearly, this is an important metric for all supply chain organizations. However, as I mentioned earlier in the book, it is not unusual for me to find companies that meet their commitments less than seventy percent of the time.

If there is a delay, do we revise the original commit date so the customer now knows when to expect it?

Whenever there is a delay from the original commit date, then it is important to revise the commit date in a separate field. Guess what this new field is labeled? You guessed it, the Revised Commit Date. The customer appreciates it when you bother to let them know when to expect shipment. However, without this field, it is typical to update the original commit date when a delay occurs. The problem with this approach is that now you have lost the ability to measure on time delivery performance versus your original commitment.

Having both fields means that you can retain the ability to measure performance, and keep the customer updated when delays occur. It can also be useful to measure on-time delivery versus the revised ship date. This does not measure how well you are meeting your commitments, but it will be an indicator of how well you inform customers when you delay an order. It is bad enough to be late, but to also not update the customer on when you will deliver their product will just make matters worse.

Chapter Summary

> **Demand Control** prevents large customer orders from consuming all inventory in your pipeline. The system holds orders when they exceed a defined threshold, so they can be reviewed before deciding what action to take.

> **Available-to-promise (ATP)** provides the ability to much more accurately predict when customers will receive their orders. Capable-to-promise (CTP) is more

applicable to an MTO environment. It is much more data-intensive than ATP.

➤ **Forecast Consumption** policies explain how customer demand will consume the forecast. The primary policies are backward consumption, forward consumption, and backward then forward consumption. The selection of consumption policy typically depends upon the number of customer orders for a given item.

➤ **Order Dates** in the system must help us answer critical questions such as on-time delivery versus customer request date and our commit date. It's important to capture the date the customer placed the order and when we delivered it, so that we can measure lead time accurately. Also, if we delay delivery, then we should update the Revised Commit Date in the system, so that we can inform customers.

Chapter 11

Forecast Accuracy

All models are wrong, but some are useful.

—George Box, British statistician

In his 1976 paper published in the Journal of the American Statistical Association, George Box famously stated, "All models are wrong, but some are useful[8]." In other words, you should never expect a completely accurate forecast, but forecasting itself is a useful exercise despite its limitations. He also said that, knowing the models are inherently wrong, we must pay attention to what about them might be wrong: "It is inappropriate to be concerned about safety from mice when there are tigers afoot." The point for those who create forecasts is that it is critical to measure forecast accuracy correctly; otherwise, you'll end up chasing mice when tigers are afoot. Mistaking the two is actually much easier than you might think. In this chapter, we will learn how to avoid this mistake.

Before we start, let me ask you a question: What do the following products have in common: gardening equipment, yeast, dumbbells, bicycles, flour, and seeds? It is difficult to imagine any common thread between these products, but there is one!

---

8   George E. P. Box, "Robustness in the strategy of scientific model building," *Robustness in Statistics*, edited by Robert L. Launer and Graham N. Wilkinson, (New York, Academic Press, 1979), 202.

The link between them is that their demand skyrocketed when COVID-19 became a pandemic and everyone had to stay at home. The situation caused people to suddenly remember how to bake, exercise, garden, and ride bikes again. People hoarded the essentials, such as toilet paper and liquor.

Everybody rightfully recognizes the huge sacrifice made by the front-line workers during this period. Another group that also endured the worst of this pandemic was the supply chain professionals who had sleepless nights trying to keep products on the shelf. Those of you who have worked in the supply chain world for even a fleeting time will know that such unforeseen events are daily occurrences. For example, a recent client of mine received unwelcome news that the US Food and Drug Administration denied their application for approval of one of their products. This news reduced projected demand for key raw materials by eighty percent overnight. Suffice to say, supply chain leaders must be on their toes, constantly assessing potential disruptions to forecasted demand.

My point is that forecast accuracy is both important and fragile and, as a result, it presents a very real risk to supply chain performance.

This chapter provides guidance on how to apply rigor to measuring forecast accuracy and the related supply chain risk. Not measuring accuracy properly is like using a GPS in a heavily built-up area. The patchy signal means that you are receiving inaccurate data on how to move forward. You end up going round in circles, and your journey becomes much longer than necessary.

Because forecasts are inherently inaccurate, we must ensure that we don't expect perfection or set unreasonable targets. Your role here is not to react to all forecast errors, because many of them will be due to random variation that is not within your control. Your challenge is to have the wisdom to know the difference between tigers and mice and the courage to fight the tigers.

It may seem that measuring forecast accuracy should be straightforward, right? At the end of the month, just compare the actual demand for an item versus its forecast. What can be so complicated about that? We will see how it is frequently unclear what we mean by demand. Not only that, but you should also expect confusion as to which forecast to use. In other words, nothing is clear, and most organizations do not measure forecast accuracy correctly, which means that we waste much time and energy. Let's drill down in more detail about which forecast to use, and how to define demand.

Forecast Offset

One day, before you begin a hike, you listen to the weather report, and you hear it will be a gloriously sunny day. You dress appropriately to keep cool, and then suddenly just thirty minutes into your hike the heavens open and it starts pouring. Needless to say, you get drenched, and you have some choice words to say about your local weather report. You get home about the same time as your partner, who has been out shopping. You notice that they were fully prepared for the nasty weather with an umbrella, a raincoat, and rain boots. You know that they left the house only an hour after you did, so you wonder how they managed to be so well prepared. They tell you that they also checked the weather report as they left the house, and it accurately predicted a heavy rainstorm. In other words, it was the timing of the forecast that made all the difference. The timing was perfect for your partner but not timely enough to save you from getting drenched.

How does this apply to supply chain management? It is not enough to just create an accurate forecast, but the timing is also critical.

For example, let's say that today is July 1 and so June has just finished. It is time to measure June's forecast accuracy. Which forecast should you use? Many organizations would use the forecast distributed closest to the start of June. Guess what? These organizations would typically be wrong! If you don't receive the accurate forecast by the right time, then your supply chain ends up not properly prepared. This will often result in unfortunate results, such as somebody getting drenched by a rainstorm. Look at the scenario below and see if you can figure out the problem:

Forecast Accuracy

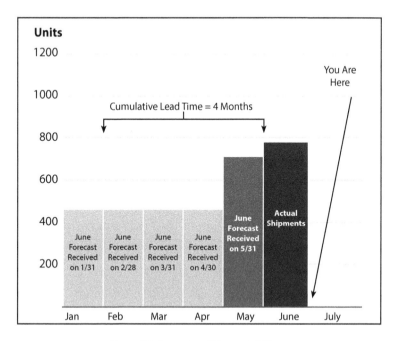

Figure 33: Example of Forecast Offset.

The first question that we must answer is when do we need to receive an accurate forecast for June demand? The answer is: by the time we must make decisions using that forecast. This is known as the cumulative lead time, which is four months in this example. This is the combined lead time from purchasing raw materials to the manufacture and shipment of your products.

The first decision would be which raw materials to purchase and how many. This means that to effectively fulfill June demand, your purchasing team must place purchase orders by the end of January. What information did the buyers have in this example? Right, that demand would be for four-hundred units. As it turns out, actual demand ended up at eight-hundred units. Ouch! I

119

hope you have some flexible suppliers that will turn on a dime for you, because you have lots of expediting to do. The forecast was only fifty percent of actual demand. The problem is that many organizations will use the latest forecast received to measure accuracy.

As you can see, the sales team eventually did predict that demand would be much higher than earlier forecasts. They increased the forecast to seven-hundred units in May, which is obviously much closer to what actually happened. If the organization made the mistake of using the forecast received in May, they would report the accuracy at eighty-six percent (700/800), which clearly does not represent the true extent of the forecast error (i.e., fifty percent).

When the "you know what" hits the fan towards the end of June and shelves became empty, many companies would not see that it was actually the forecast that was at the root of their problem. The bottom line is that which forecast to use in the accuracy calculation matters very much.

HOW DO WE DEFINE DEMAND?

The second question is, what do we mean by demand? For example, in the scenario below, in which month did the demand occur:

Forecast Accuracy

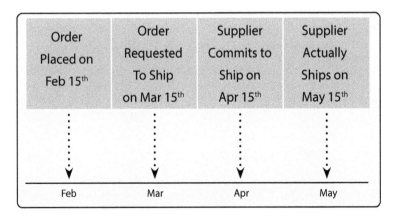

Figure 34: Demand date possibilities.

Which of the following four options would you select?

Ship Date (May 15)

Companies will frequently define demand as when they ship the product. However, there is one major flaw in that approach: What if the order doesn't ship until weeks after the customer actually wanted the product due to a supply shortage? In this case, in using the ship date, you are not measuring the demand date; you are measuring when you were able to *supply* the demand.

Commit date (April 15)

What if the supplier uses the date that they committed to ship the order? Again, if the supplier could not commit to the date that the customer requested shipment of their order, they fall into the trap of confusing demand with supply availability.

Order date (February 15)

Alternatively, we could use the date that the customer placed their order. The problem here though is that the customer places their order on February 15, but they do not want it until March 15. By using the order date, we inaccurately report the demand data in February when it is actually in March.

Request date (March 15)

March is when the customer requested the product, and this is the best practice. The demand date should be when the customer wants the order. Unfortunately, many organizations do not accurately capture the requested date. For example, the customer may request the order to ship tomorrow, even though your standard lead time is three business days. Unless we develop policies for such situations, then the request date data could be completely useless.

In this case, when the request date data is inaccurate (or missing), we must select an alternative date based upon your situation.

For example, if customers always want their product as soon as they place their order, then the order date and request date are the same date. In that case, the order date, February 15, will work fine. Alternatively, if your on-time delivery rate versus the request date is upward of ninety-eight percent, then the ship date, May 15, is a good substitute. Similarly, if you typically commit orders by the request date, then you could use the commit date, April 15.

Now that we have a better understanding of the key data required to calculate forecast accuracy, we will look at how we use these inputs to calculate accuracy.

Forecast Accuracy Calculation

We can start with the simple scenario below:

Item	Demand		Net Differences	Absolute Differences
	Forecasted	Actual		
A	100	0	100	100
B	0	100	-100	100
Total	100	100	0	200

Table 6: Example: Simplified Forecast Accuracy calculation.

If this inaccuracy level is causing painful flashbacks, then please lay down and take a nap. It will be alright, I promise! If your organization would consider this situation as a 100 percent accurate forecast, I send my commiserations. Yes, the total forecast and total actual demand were both 100 units. Obviously, there is a slight flaw in that logic! In this scenario, item A is gathering dust on the shelf, and we can't obtain item B.

Going back to the weather example, it is as if we forecasted rain for ten hours on Saturday, and on Sunday we did not forecast any rain. Based upon this forecast, you planned to binge- watch your favorite TV show on Saturday and scheduled a barbeque with friends on Sunday to take advantage of the projected, glorious sunshine. But in reality, it did not rain on Saturday at

Lean Forecasting Demystified

all, and it rained for ten hours on Sunday. On Monday, you turn on the news and they brag about the fact that they predicted ten hours of rain, and that is what we got—who cares if they got the days mixed up? All your friends cared, because they were stuck watching TV with you on Sunday because it was too wet to be outside.

ABSOLUTE DIFFERENCE

This is where the "absolute difference" concept becomes especially useful. The absolute difference is just the size of the gap between two numbers, regardless of direction:

Item	Demand		Net Differences	Absolute Differences
	Forecasted	Actual		
A	100	0	100	100
B	0	100	-100	100
Total	100	100	0	200

Table 7: Example: Forecast Accuracy using absolute differences.

This table now tells the more accurate story that the total forecast error was 200, not zero. Is this error level acceptable? Since we always expect some error, we need to be able to compare the forecast error to the total forecast. In this case, the forecast was 100 units, and the forecast error was 200 units, so no, this amount of error is unacceptable. But how do we quantify the accuracy level? This is where mean absolute percent error (MAPE) can be a useful metric.

124

Forecast Accuracy

Mean Absolute Percent Error (MAPE)

The most popular forecast accuracy measure is MAPE. It
measures the percent absolute error, thereby taking into
consideration the gap size in relation to the forecast. Obviously,
a 200-unit absolute error is much better if the total forecast was
for 10,000 versus 100 units. Once we have calculated the percent
error for every item, then we can calculate the mean percent
error, as follows:

$$\frac{\text{Abs Difference x 100}}{\text{Actual Demand}}$$

See the example below:

Item	Demand		Net Differences	Absolute Differences	Percent Error
	Forecasted	Actual			
A	50	60	-10	10	17%
B	120	90	30	30	33%
Total	170	150	20	40	25%

Table 8: MAPE calculation

Item A had a 17 percent error and item B had a 33 percent error,
so the average error was 25 percent.

There are many different methods for calculating forecast errors,
but MAPE is the most popular.

What is a Good MAPE?

As discussed earlier, technically, there is no right answer to this question. Demand volatility has the primary impact on MAPE. Obviously, less predictable demand will cause higher MAPE, and more demand predictability will cause lower MAPE levels. A better practice is to compare your forecast to the MAPE for the naive forecast, because it has the same demand volatility level. As such, it is a more valid comparison to the forecast for which we have spent time and effort. In other words, a good MAPE is one that is better than the naive forecast.

But, if you really want numbers, from my experience, the following MAPE levels can be taken as rough guidelines:

MAPE	Interpretation
<10	Highly Accurate Forecasting
10-20	Good Forecasting
20-50	Reasonable Forecasting
>50	Inaccurate Forecasting

Table 9: Interpretation of MAPE levels.

The other factor to consider when evaluating your MAPE is, how is it trending? In other words, set MAPE targets based upon your starting point. Use your previous performance as a benchmark. Typically, if there has not been a concerted effort previously to improve forecast accuracy, it should be a target rich environment—like fishing in a barrel!

Improving MAPE

As discussed earlier, reducing artificial volatility is the most effective approach to improved forecast accuracy. I would also add one more approach: root cause analysis. Identify the items with the largest percent error and find out what caused the discrepancy between actual and forecasted demand. The more discrepancies that you investigate, the better you will understand chronic issues that are plaguing your ability to improve accuracy.

How to Convert Forecast Inaccuracy Data to Safety Stock Levels

Unfortunately, even if we become forecasting savants, we will always have forecast errors. The only questions are: how inaccurate, and how do we prevent these errors from interfering with service levels to our customers? Once you have calculated how much actual demand differs from your forecast, it is possible to calculate how much buffer to build in to *minimize* stockouts. I stress the word "minimize" because it is impossible to eliminate stockouts completely. However, you can set service level targets to estimate how often stockouts will occur. We should note that the required safety stock level grows exponentially as the desired service level increases.

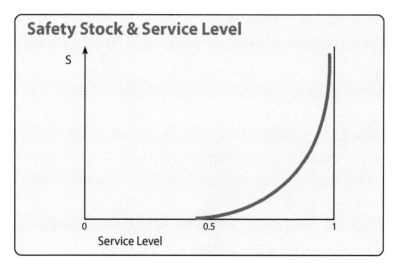

Figure 35: Safety stock and service level.

For example, the buffer required to achieve 98 percent service level is 25 percent higher than that required to achieve 95 percent performance. In supply chain speak, this buffer is known as *safety stock*. Without safety stock, your organization is burying its head in the sand. You are assuming a perfect world, and those of you who have worked in the supply chain world for ten seconds will know that is not true. For example, if an item had a forecast of 100 units, and you actually sold 101 units, you would expect to experience a backorder if you did decide against safety stock.

Realistically, if the forecast is 100 units, you would expect to sell more than 100 units 50 percent of the time, and less than 100 units 50 percent of the time. Which means that without a safety stock, your supply chain will experience stockouts an estimated 50 percent of the time. If that is your supply chain strategy—good luck!

In my experience, most organizations do have safety stock, set at an arbitrary level, with no understanding of the level of demand variation.

I am willing to bet that many of you work in an organization where you spread safety stock level evenly, like peanut butter, across all items. For example, the safety stock for every finished goods item is set to three-months' demand. As you will learn below, the peanut butter approach is not optimal, to say the least.

The better practice is to calculate safety stock based upon three key variables: desired service level, demand variance, and lead time variance. I will not get into the algebraic formula too deeply (you're welcome). For those of you in the math nerd club, of which I am an honorary member, please refer to Peter Ling's article referenced in the "Recommended Reading" section at the end of the book.

DEMAND VARIABILITY

Demand variability is the primary determinant of safety stock levels. More variability, more safety stock. We often use demand variability and desired service level to calculate safety stock requirements.

We measure demand variability by calculating what is known as standard deviation. Once you have measured the standard deviation of your historical data, the next step is to define your desired service level. The table below shows the relationship between service level and what is known as the *Z score*. Without getting too technical, the Z score measures how many standard deviations a data point is from the mean. In other words, if we want better service levels, larger safety stocks are required to cover demand that is further from average demand.

Service Level	Z Score
95%	1.645
96%	1.751
97%	1.881
98%	2.054
99%	2.326

Table 10: Z scores for service levels.

Simply multiply the standard deviation by the Z score and voilà, you have calculated the level of safety stock required based upon the level of variation in demand.

For example, if the standard deviation of demand were 10.0 and you wish to achieve a 95 percent service level, multiply 10 x 1.645 (Z score). In this case, the optimal safety stock level to buffer against demand variation is 16.45 (or round up to seventeen units). Unfortunately, demand variation is not the only uncertainty in the supply chain; there is also lead time variability.

LEAD TIME VARIABILITY

I know that this will not be a surprise to anyone, but sometimes suppliers do not deliver on time (I can hear you thinking, *Thanks, Captain Obvious.*) What I advise clients to do is to calculate average lead time based upon historical data and compare it to the longest lead time.

For example, item DFG000 has an average lead time of six weeks and its highest lead time during the selected period was ten weeks, which is a four-week difference. If you take this data at face value, you will add four weeks of safety stock to buffer against that uncertainty. But we should apply common sense here. What if we had received the item 100 times, and every other delivery had been within six weeks? I suggest that you investigate the outlier to see if it was a one-off before adding four weeks' worth of inventory. If supplier delays are typically no more than a couple of days, then don't worry about it. However, if these delays tend to be longer, then add more safety stock to account for these delays. For example, say you look at the data and conclude that it is very unusual for the supplier to be more than two weeks late. If the weekly demand was 100 units, then it would make sense to add 200 units to the safety stock already calculated based upon demand variance.

Chapter Summary

➤ The recent pandemic was an extreme example of **unforeseen demand disruption**, which occurs every day in the supply chain world. Since the accuracy of the forecast is critical to supply chain performance, this uncertainty presents a substantial risk.

➤ **Forecast Offset:** Not only must the forecast be accurate, but it must be accurate when we make important decisions regarding purchase commitments. We use the cumulative lead time of the end-to-end supply chain to determine which forecast to use to measure forecast accuracy.

➤ There are several choices for which **demand date** to use in the forecast accuracy calculation. These choices include order date, request date, commit date, or ship date. In general, the request date is the best measure of when the customer "demanded" the product. If the request date is not available, then we can select one of the other options depending upon the circumstances.

➤ The most common forecast accuracy metric is **mean absolute percent error (MAPE),** which we calculate by measuring the absolute difference between the forecast and actual demand. Then divide the difference by actual demand and multiply by 100 to calculate the absolute percent error. Finally, by calculating the average percent error for all items, we can calculate MAPE.

➤ **MAPE targets** should be based upon improvements from current MAPE levels and not external benchmarking, since MAPE is dependent upon demand variation, which is typically outside our control.

➤ **To improve MAPE,** we can employ the standard root cause analysis approach. In other words, calculate which items have the most errors, and what the reason was for the error. Then use the 80/20 rule to identify and address the few critical systemic issues.

➤ Once we have quantified forecast accuracy levels, we can use them to measure how much **safety stock** is necessary to buffer against these errors to minimize stockouts. In addition, we require lead time variation and desired service levels for this calculation.

Chapter 12

Forecast Bias

Making a wrong decision is understandable. Refusing to search continually for learning is not.

—Phillip B. Crosby, American quality guru

I once worked for a start-up company in the renewable energy industry, which was in the process of securing another round of funding from investors. To help sell the deal, executives gave incentives to the sales team to obtain orders from its distributors. These distributors then sold directly to consumers. These orders were meant to be a signal to investors that their product was flying off the shelves, and they could barely keep up with demand. In turn, the objective was to encourage investors to fund a three-times expansion of manufacturing capacity at its contract manufacturers. And it worked!

When I started, the client was installing and validating machinery, and the good times were about to roll. There was only one small fly in the ointment. **The products were not flying off the shelves; in fact, they were barely moving at all.**

The problem was that while they were giving distributors deep discounts to purchase products, the consumers were not buying at anywhere near the same rate. In other words, inventory was building up at the distributors to the point that their warehouses were overflowing, and they could not accept more deliveries.

In fact, in all the chaos, the distributor turned away several deliveries. The channel was well and truly stuffed!

Unfortunately, the distributor purchase orders were non-binding, so they began to cancel their orders, just as the new capacity was coming onboard. My client had encouraged the contract manufacturer to hire enough workers to run all the new machines. But instead of increased throughput, all the canceled orders meant that machines were sitting idle. I calculated that it would take more than six months to reduce inventory to an acceptable level at the distributors.

Once reality set in, my client slashed production rates and laid off many employees. This would have been avoidable if not for an extreme case of forecast bias.

This company was by no means the only organization participating in such antics. In my experience, forecast bias is the one practice that causes more unnecessary waste than all others. In this case, it was a positive forecast bias in that the sales forecast was much higher than the actual demand. The result was excess inventory, high capital costs, unnecessary hiring/firing, organizational stress, low cash flow, and high transportation costs.

Target Practice

The bottom line is that forecast bias is bad, and worse than that, it is completely avoidable. Before I explain how to avoid it, I would like to use the target practice diagram below to illustrate what we mean by forecast bias and how it differs from your typical forecast error, otherwise known as random variation.

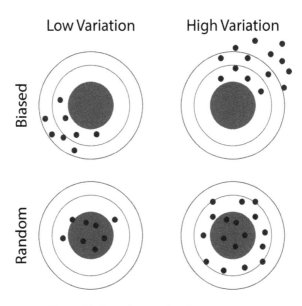

Figure 36: Biased vs. random forecast error.

As you can see, we clustered our shots on the top two targets on one side. The ones on the left side are all grouped at about eight o'clock, and on the right side we clumped them together at about one o'clock. For some reason, the shooters had biases. This is different on the bottom two targets. In these cases, we randomly distributed our shots around the target, and we did not cluster them in one area. These targets also illustrate that variation is a completely different concept than bias. Variation just describes how close to the center of the target the shots are. In other words, how precise are they? It is possible that the shots are both biased but also very precise, so they are all close to the target's middle but grouped together in one area.

Now that we better understand bias, we should also know that there are two types: positive and negative. Positive bias means that the forecasts are frequently above actual demand, and conversely, negative bias is when forecasts are typically below actual demand. In the section below, we'll look at what causes these biases. Then, at the end of the chapter, I'll share some tips on how we may remove bias.

Positive Bias

Aggressive Management Targets

The primary reason for positive forecast bias is that management creates aggressive revenue targets. The company divides its total revenue forecast across regions or business units, and eventually, each salesperson has a considerable number to meet. Typically, when confronted with this situation, salespeople will not blink and will just nod their heads in acceptance. We know what happens to the messenger of unwelcome news, right? Inevitably, actual sales will mostly fall short of the forecast, resulting in excess inventory and waste.

New Product Introductions

Have you ever heard of Cheetos lip balm? No, I suspected not. In 2005, Frito-Lay decided that since their Cheetos were so popular, how about introducing a lip balm flavored like Cheetos? The company expected loyal fans to be excited for the product, but who would have guessed it would be a flop? The company quickly pulled it from shelves. My experience has been that forecasts for new product introductions can be wildly optimistic.

With all the resources spent developing a new product, there tends to be an irrational exuberance about the potential popularity of the new product. As we have discussed, even when there is no shortage of historical demand data, forecast accuracy is by no means guaranteed. Then, it should be no surprise that projecting demand for new products is even more challenging. It is all too easy for an organization to convince itself that their product will be the best thing since sliced bread. Unfortunately, demand frequently does not meet these elevated expectations, and they must hurriedly scale back the supply chain.

FEAR OF STOCKOUTS

Off-brand stores such as TJ Maxx, HomeGoods, and Marshalls love it when brands over-purchase. These stores buy up excess inventory at a steep discount from traditional brands to sell in their stores. This is a business model based upon the expectation that these brands will over-purchase inventory. Why? Brands live in fear of stockouts. Not only do they have revenue loss, but they also create frustrated customers, impact on brand reputation, and the cost to expedite the next shipment. Intrinsically, therefore, the organization is naturally inclined to pad the forecast to reduce the probability of stockouts.

IMPRESS WALL STREET

At the start of the chapter, I told the story about the start-up company that was overly optimistic in their sales predictions to influence further investment in the company. This can also be true of publicly traded firms who know that news of reduced sales will undoubtedly impact share price. So, they maintain their upbeat forecast for as long as possible, despite the negative consequences of excess inventory and increased costs.

Negative Bias

In the nineteenth century, people often used sandbags as a weapon to attack somebody. Eventually, people used the term *sandbagging* to describe someone that ambushed another person. It then evolved to describe a poker player who would ambush other players by betting low at first, in the hope of placing large bets later in the hand.

Supply chain professionals now use sandbagging to describe a situation in which somebody deliberately creates a forecast lower than what they really think will happen. Hence, a forecast with a negative bias has also become known as sandbagging. Just like positive bias, there are several reasons for this practice.

FORECAST-BASED BONUS PLANS

Management often inadvertently encourages this behavior by setting quarterly milestones and bonus plans based upon sales forecasts. Thus, it is in the sales team's best interest to submit the lowest defendable forecast. By setting the bar as low as possible, the chances of exceeding the forecast become much higher, and the sales team gets to pad their bank accounts. In this case, constant inventory shortages will occur, thereby impacting deliveries to customers.

REDUCED PRESSURE

In many organizations, the sales team is under constant pressure to meet revenue targets. Therefore, in some situations it is tempting to submit a lower forecast, which, if accepted, will tend to result in less pressure and management attention during the forecast period. Constant pressure can be extremely stressful, so again, it does not encourage the sales team to submit aggressive forecasts.

Forecast Bias

Missing Demand Sources

As mentioned earlier, sometimes certain demand sources are missing from the forecast, especially NRG demand such as internal demand from engineering and R&D. These internal users sometimes have access to inventory that is allocated to external customers. I have seen warehouse managers add security gates to prevent inventory from "walking off the shelf." Alternatively, I have seen buyers lock away scarce items in their cubicles to ensure that the production line does not run out. Why can't we all just get along?

This explains many reasons that bias often exists in forecasts, causing unnecessary inaccuracy. As you see, forecast bias is very disruptive, and the worst part of it is that it is completely within management's control. Therefore, unlike random variation, the target for forecast bias should be **zero**!

How Do We Calculate Forecast Bias?

Now that we know more about forecast bias, the next step will be how to calculate it. Unfortunately, this will require a little mathematics.

To determine forecast bias, we must calculate the **running sum of forecast error (RSFE).** We can simply calculate RSFE by summing up the difference between the *aggregated sales forecast* and the *actual demand* over a twelve-month period.

For example, in Table 12 below page 141 you can see that in the previous twelve months, we forecasted 292,168 units and sold 309,887. In other words, the RSFE is 17,719 units

(309,887-292,168). If there is a major difference between the
two numbers, then you know that you have bias.

Obviously, it is very unlikely that the forecast and actual demand
will exactly match up, so just because there is a difference
does not automatically indicate bias. How large a difference is
significant? Where do we draw the line between insignificant
and significant bias? Is a 17,719-difference significant? The
percentage error matters. If the total forecast were three million,
then a difference of less than 20,000 units would seem trivial,
right? In terms of percentage, it is about 0.6 percent, which most
organizations would greet with high fives.

However, in this case, the difference is about 6.1 percent (see
Table 12 below). Not as good as 0.6 percent, but does it signify
bias? I know the suspense must be killing you, but you will find
out soon enough. We must start by calculating the mean absolute
deviation (MAD), which measures the amount of random
variation.

Mean Absolute Deviation (MAD)

Higher absolute deviation signifies more random variation
between forecast and actual demand. MAD is simply the average
absolute deviation in the dataset. As you can see from Table
13 on page 141, the total absolute deviation is 35,415, over
the twelve-month period. In which case, the MAD is 2,951
(35,415/12). Why is this important? Because it puts the RSFE in
perspective. As discussed earlier in the book, higher variation is
more challenging to forecast, so it matters how RSFE compares
to MAD. We refer to this comparison as the *tracking signal*.

Forecast Bias

	Jan-17	Feb-17	Mar-17	Apr-17	May-17	Jun-17	Jul-17	Aug-17	Sep-17	Oct-17	Nov-17	Dec-17	Total
Forecast	17,469	27,364	21,435	22,023	22,554	23,059	22,937	34,045	21,247	24,475	27,442	28,118	292,168
Actual Demand	21,066	27,277	21,113	28,494	24,607	23,123	24,342	29,024	33,026	24,929	28,186	24,700	309,887

Table 11: Forecast vs. demand.

	Jan-17	Feb-17	Mar-17	Apr-17	May-17	Jun-17	Jul-17	Aug-17	Sep-17	Oct-17	Nov-17	Dec-17
Forecast	17,469	27,364	21,435	22,023	22,554	23,059	22,937	34,045	21,247	24,475	27,442	28,118
Actual Demand	21,066	27,277	21,113	28,494	24,607	23,123	24,342	29,024	33,026	24,929	28,186	24,700
RSFE	(3,597)	(3,510)	(3,188)	(9,659)	(11,712)	(11,776)	(13,181)	(8,160)	(19,939)	(20,393)	(21,137)	(17,719)
% difference	-20.6%	-7.8%	-4.8%	-10.9%	-10.6%	-8.8%	-8.4%	-4.3%	-9.4%	-8.6%	-8.0%	-6.1%

Table 12: Forecast vs. demand, with running sum of forecast error (RSFE) included.

	Jan-17	Feb-17	Mar-17	Apr-17	May-17	Jun-17	Jul-17	Aug-17	Sep-17	Oct-17	Nov-17	Dec-17	Total
Forecast	17,469	27,364	21,435	22,023	22,554	23,059	22,937	34,045	21,247	24,475	27,442	28,118	292,168
Actual Demand	21,066	27,277	21,113	28,494	24,607	23,123	24,342	29,024	33,026	24,929	28,186	24,700	309,887
Abs Difference	3,597	87	322	6,471	2,053	64	1,405	5,021	11,779	454	744	3,418	35,415

Table 13: Forecast vs. demand, with mean absolute difference (MAD) included.

TRACKING SIGNAL

The tracking signal determines if the MAD is significant relative to the RSFE.

Tracking Signal = 3 x MAD = 3 x 2,951 = 8,853

The tracking signals are the guardrails. In this case the upper limit is +8.853 and the lower limit is -8,853. Once we bypass them, we are in "bias" territory, which is a dangerous place to be.

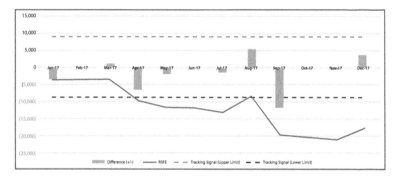

Figure 37: Mapping the tracking signal.

In the diagram above, the red lines denote the high and low tracking signals (guardrails), which are three times MAD above and below the mean. In this case, we can see that RSFE drifts into "enemy territory," telling us that there is indeed a significant bias to the forecast. Because the RSFE line is **below** the tracking signal, we also know there is a negative bias. In this situation, it would then be good practice to drill down further by region, sales territory, SKU, etc.—whatever makes sense for your organization—to identify the source(s) of the bias.

Removing Bias

Remember, all that bias exists due to management practices. Therefore, it will not be productive to talk to the sales team directly to correct this bias. How to approach management will differ depending upon your organization. If you can present the negative impact that bias has on supply chain performance, you can influence this bad practice. If all else fails, you could automatically increase or decrease your forecast by the bias factor. In the example above, that would mean increasing whatever forecast you receive by 6.1 percent. This is not the best practice, since there are now two forecasts floating around the organization, so this should be your last resort.

Chapter Summary

> **Positive forecast bias** occurs when the forecast is consistently above actual demand. Examples of why it happens include management setting aggressive targets, ambitious new product introductions, attempts to impress investors, and concerns about stockouts.

> **Negative forecast bias** (sandbagging) occurs when the forecast is consistently below actual demand. Examples of why this occurs include using forecasts to calculate bonuses, attempts to reduce management pressure, and missing forecast sources.

> To determine whether forecast bias exists in your organization, first calculate the **running sum of the forecast error (RSFE).** In other words, compare the

total forecast to actual demand over an extended period, such as twelve months.

➤ Next, find the **mean absolute deviation (MAD):** Calculate the absolute variance each month, total these variances, and divide by the total months.

➤ Using the MAD value, calculate the **tracking signal** (guardrails) and see whether the RSFE exceeds the tracking signal. If it does, the bias in your forecasts is significant.

➤ **Bad management practices** create forecast bias, so we must address it at the top levels of the organization.

Chapter 13

Optimizing Forecast Software

Oh, what a tangled web we weave.

—Sir Walter Scott, Scottish historian and novelist

At some point, your organization will believe that forecast software will be the answer to all your prayers. This could well be the case, but from my experience, it is quite possible that it will cause more problems, complexity, time, and expense. This chapter is dedicated to highlighting the potential pitfalls.

Garbage In, Garbage Out (GIGO)

A pharmaceutical client asked me to investigate why they had delayed the implementation of a supply chain planning software project by several months. The project's goal was to develop business analytics, leveraging the outputs from their planning tool. As an example, if the software were working correctly, it would project inventory available over the planning horizon. This was particularly interesting to finance since they could use the data to calculate projected inventory turnover. However, I very quickly discovered one major glitch in this plan. The planners were not using the software for planning purposes. This project was the poster child for "garbage in, garbage out." The third-party developer was quite happy to take the company's money as it built these useless reports.

My next assignment was to figure out when the reports *would* provide useful information. Those of you familiar with the planning process will understand that accurate outputs require several accurate inputs. But, even before that, we must define and align the business process with the software functionality. It is the business process that defines the data required. Planning processes as a whole will definitely require accurate inventory, bills of material, and purchase orders. For these inputs to be reliable, they require accurate and timely transactions in the system by many different groups. Unfortunately, I found little buy-in from these other departments, which meant that it would be a long time before these reports would be of any use. In fact, it actually took another two years before the planning software and data were ready for use.

The takeaway here is that it is critical to validate that your organization is ready before embarking upon the implementation of a new software.

User Requirements

At the end of the project described above, I led a post-project "lessons learned" exercise to help ascertain why adoption was so delayed. There were several significant findings, but I would like to focus on one here—namely that the team submitted incomplete user requirements.

Since the team had only ever planned in spreadsheets, they could not articulate their requirements in "software speak." In terms of available functionality, they didn't know what they didn't know. Since they had not requested much necessary functionality, it was not clear if the functionality existed or not. If it did not exist, the next question would be whether there was an effective workaround.

For example, for a pharmaceutical company, the ability to consider expiration dates is essential. Not only that, but customers will require a minimum remaining shelf life (MRSL). The team had included the expiration date requirement, but nobody had thought to add the MRSL requirements.

As a result, the planning calculation still thought that batches were shippable, even when they had insufficient remaining shelf-life days. As you can see in the example below, this can make a significant difference. In this case, a batch will expire in eight months but is only shippable for six months. If we project that we will consume the batch within the next six months, then there is nothing to worry about. But what if we will not consume the inventory by month six? Then our planning system will think that you still have until the end of month eight to have a new batch available, when you really need it two months earlier.

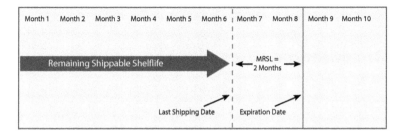

Figure 38: Minimum remaining shelf life.

Fortunately, there was a workaround, but it would require some IT development time. Since they had already implemented the software, however, there were no IT resources assigned to the project. The development work eventually happened, but not until IT delayed it. By that point, it was difficult for the planners to trust the software results again.

Conversely, the team also submitted user requirements beyond the organization's capability. If you have participated in any software implementation, you will be familiar with the fact that some users will create an idealistic wish list. The problem is that even if the software had the capability, it still required mature business processes, strong cross-functional alignment, and valid data.

For example, in the world of supply chain planning, statistical forecasting can add much value. On the other hand, it requires lots of effort. We must cleanse historical shipment data, train planners, and establish and manage adoption of cross-functional policies. In other words, this is not a trivial undertaking! In effect, it is a project unto itself, on top of the software implementation. Since these projects are often competing for the same resources, we must be realistic about Phase 1 scope. Challenge the organization and the software on its ability to meet the requirements.

Organizational Commitment

The key lesson here is that your software implementation will fail if your organization is not committed to the work required. Management may have been seduced by the promise of wonderfully accurate forecasts immediately after we launch the software. It is important, therefore, to manage expectations from the start. As we have discussed, demand volatility has the largest impact on accuracy. There is only so much that a software can achieve. In fact, the software implementation could have been completely successful, but management perception is that it was a failure because it did not move the needle far enough in terms of forecast accuracy.

It is also very possible that we will fail to install the software. This tends to happen when management underestimates the effort required to not only install the software, but also to ensure sufficiently accurate data. In addition, the organization can belatedly figure out that the software is overly complicated or is missing key functionality. This often happens when the user community was not sufficiently engaged during the selection process. For example, one client had two very distinct distribution channels: wholesale and direct shipping. For several reasons, it was important to be able to forecast these channels separately. However, the implementation team missed this critical requirement. The workarounds were so cumbersome, that they eventually resorted to spreadsheets again.

Here are a few questions to help identify potential pitfalls:

> ➤ Are team members full-time or are they still required to perform their day jobs? The risk with part-time project members is that their full-time job is their priority, so when it gets busy, the project suffers.

- ➤ Are issues resolved immediately with the support of senior management? If we bury them in notes somewhere, then we will compromise the quality of project deliverables.

- ➤ Was a thorough proof of concept conducted as part of the software selection process? This will help set expectations related to forecast performance with the new software.

Finally, if effective business processes do not exist, then it will take some effort and organizational maturity to design, develop, and deploy them. These processes will include maintaining master data, new product setup, discontinuation of old products, and so on.

A Better Approach

Now that we know where the potential landmines have been hidden, let's discuss a more effective approach. The first step is to design the end-to-end forecasting business process.

Each step of the business process will include the activity, the role responsible for performing the step, and the system. Your team will map out the current process and list all the pain points associated with it. Then, map out the ideal state—one that minimizes waste, removes pain points, and maximizes value. This ideal state is very aspirational, but it is a great practice to have this as your "north star." That way, the team does not limit itself to incrementalism by merely seeking ways to modify the current state. In other words, work from the ideal state backward, rather than the current state forward.

The next step is to list all the activities required to get to the ideal state. We must now prioritize these activities, based upon impact and effort. We will score each activity from one to five on each axis:

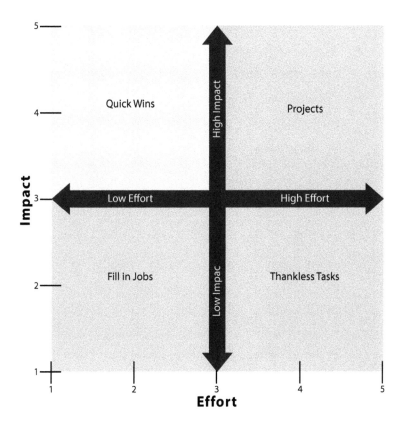

Figure 39: Impact vs Effort matrix.

IMPACT

In terms of impact, start with the end in mind. What is your primary objective and how will you measure it? We can then assess each activity against its potential impact on these metrics.

Effort

How much effort do we require to manage each new practice? We can define effort by:

- ➤ Amount of data required
- ➤ Number of departments required to align on the practice and resistance level
- ➤ Complexity of the process
  - ◆ We must train the team to understand and manage the process.

Now that each potential solution has a score, in terms of impact and effort, we can plot them on the diagram above.

Here is a brief description of possible actions in each quadrant:

- ➤ **Quick wins** are actions that should definitely be in Phase 1. In fact, it could be that some of these activities do not require a software solution. For example, we can develop a relationship with a large, willing customer to level load demand without any technology requirements.

- ➤ **Projects** are initiatives that require significant resources but offer a worthwhile return on this investment. It is typical to find that twenty percent of the projects have the potential to have eighty percent of the impact. We should identify these projects and allocate resources to them. The goal is to include these projects in Phase 1.

- ➤ **Fill-in jobs** are initiatives that you should undertake if there are no more quick wins or projects. Alternatively, it may be possible to expand the scope of a project, so that it addresses one or more fill-in jobs.

> **Thankless tasks** do not offer enough benefit for the effort required.

The quick wins and projects should be the primary basis for the user requirements. They will not get you to the "ideal state," but you will be much closer once the software implementation is complete. Finally, create your "Future State 1.0" process map, including all these Phase 1 solutions.

Now that we know how to prioritize user requirements, let's review a **few critical tools and practices** included in this book, as well as important functionality to request in a supply chain planning or forecasting software:

Abnormal Demand

Statistical forecasting relies upon historical demand to calculate future demand. But to be accurate, ideally, you would want to know if there was any abnormal demand during this period.

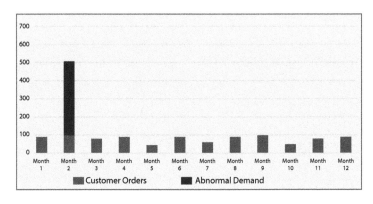

Figure 40: Abnormal demand.

For example, say your customer opens a new distribution center. There will be additional demand for a period as they stock up. You would not want to include this one-off demand in your demand history. The ability to tag these abnormal orders, therefore, can be an extremely helpful tool. There is not too much effort required, except to ensure that there is sufficient internal communication on these abnormal orders.

One of my clients had a major recall of one of its products due to quality issues. As soon as we addressed the quality issues, they had to replace them all. This caused a major demand spike, qualifying these orders as abnormal demand.

Forecast Consumption Rules

As discussed earlier in the book, forecast consumption policies explain how customer demand will consume the system forecast. The only question is, how will this happen? The primary policies are backward consumption, forward consumption, and backward then forward consumption. It is best to proactively select a policy that works for your organization and not rely upon the system default method.

Once the team has agreed upon the consumption policy, you must configure your software. If you have some definite requirements related to forecast consumption, ensure that you document them.

Available-to-Promise (ATP)

To recap, ATP functionality provides the ability to much more accurately predict when customers will receive their orders.

CTP is more applicable to an MTO environment and is much more data-intensive than ATP. This functionality typically exists within the order management module of an ERP system. When you enter a customer order, the system will calculate whether sufficient inventory is available to meet the customer's request date. This calculation typically considers inventory on hand and existing customer orders. Advanced applications will consider open replenishment orders from internal manufacturing or suppliers. Alternatively, a standard lead time will be set per item, so if inventory is unavailable, the system will apply this standard lead time to calculate the committed ship date.

Minimum Remaining Shelf Life (MRSL)

MRSL will define how many days before the expiration date you can ship the product to a customer. We will not consider inventory that is already past MRSL in the ATP calculation and will not be allocated to ship to a customer. It is important to understand your requirements related to this functionality. Obviously, if your products do not have shelf lives, you can move on. However, if your products do have shelf lives, then you need to know if the MRSL is consistent for all customers and for all items. This will determine the complexity of your MRSL requirements.

Dynamic Safety Stock

	Month 0	Month 1	Month 2	Month 3	Month 4	Month 5	Month 6	Month 7	Month 8	Month 9	Month 10
Original forecast		100	200	300	400	500	600	700	800	900	1000
Safety stock level	600	900	1200	1500	1800	2100	2400	2700	3000	3300	2300

Table 14: Dynamic safety stock.

Many organizations prefer a dynamic safety stock to a fixed one. If this is the case for your organization, make sure it is on your requirements list. A dynamic safety stock will typically change throughout the planning time fence, based upon future demand. If your product demand is trending upwards or downwards, or if demand is seasonal, then the ability for the system to adjust safety stock levels according to future demand can be beneficial. The alternative is a fixed safety stock, which will maintain the same value throughout the time fence. Obviously, this will cause excess inventory or shortages depending upon the situation.

Multiple Series

There are many potential sources for a forecast. You could statistically calculate or obtain the forecast from several parts of the organization: sales, marketing, supply chain, finance, etc. It could also be a consensus forecast, in which each team has had the opportunity to give its opinion during the sales and operations planning process. It would be good practice to evaluate the relative accuracy of these forecasts over a period of time. To support this goal, it is helpful if your forecasting software can store multiple forecasts for the same item for any given month. Ensure that you document this requirement if applicable. A word of caution: This functionality is very data-intensive since it exponentially increases the amount of data that you must manage. Be doubly sure that your organization is capable before attempting to manage multiple series.

Chapter Summary

➤ **User requirements** must be complete for successful software implementation, but also realistic relative to the organization's capability.

➤ **Software implementation** will fail if your organization is not committed to the work required.

➤ **Manage expectations** so management understands the level of improved forecast accuracy we can achieve from software alone.

➤ **Management support** is critical for success.

➤ **Develop a current state** business process map.

➤ **Redesign the future state** process, starting with the ideal state. Prioritize activities and differentiate quick wins from projects.

➤ Understand **key potential software functionality**. Evaluate software packages and their ability to meet your key requirements.

Chapter 14

Case Study

Without execution, vision is just another word for hallucination.

—Mark V. Hurd, former CEO, Oracle

In this chapter, you will learn how the practices in this book actually work in the real world. I am sure it is a relief to have reached the penultimate chapter. I will present a case study, which is actually an amalgam of my experiences with several clients to cover as many tools and practices as possible from this book.

Background

My client manufactured instruments for the medical device industry to diagnose conditions such as diabetes. For example, whenever your doctor takes a blood sample and sends it to a lab, there is a fair chance that the sample will be tested using this instrument. Not only does my client manufacture the instruments, but they also make the consumables, too. In this case, the consumables are mostly kits of specialty chemicals. The lab will mix chemicals with your blood sample to diagnose whether you have a specific medical condition.

My client's inventory has doubled over the past two years, which is now causing a cash flow issue. The good news was that the extra inventory improved their ability to ship on time to customers. Now, they wish to maintain this customer service level but with much less inventory. They identified that improved forecast accuracy is the key to achieving both the desired on-time delivery and improved inventory turns.

For this engagement, we used my "Mine the Gaps" model, which I believed would be a great fit for this initiative. This framework was the subject of my first book, which you can find in the "Recommended Reading" section at the end of the book.

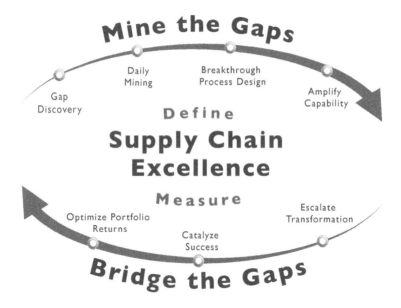

Define Excellence

This methodology starts with *defining supply chain excellence* through selection of the strategic objective and the metric to measure progress along your journey until you reach your target destination.

MINE THE GAPS

First, *Gap Discovery* leverages forecast error data to help identify key root causes. Next, *Daily Mining* will monitor performance to quickly address forecast-related issues, while also identifying ongoing chronic issues. Then, *Breakthrough Process Design* will redesign forecast-related processes for long-term, scalable change. Finally, *Amplify Capability* compares current state to best practices to select those that offer the largest impact, from which we can develop a strategic roadmap.

BRIDGE THE GAPS

In this phase, we assess, prioritize, and implement solutions to address organizational needs. The process has three steps: *Escalate Transformation,* by enacting quick wins; *Catalyze Success* through selection and execution of impactful rapid improvement workshops, otherwise known as kaizen events; and finally, *Optimize Portfolio Returns* through robust project selection techniques, allowing us to realize intended benefits through project management best practices.

Now, let's drill down into the details. Sit back, relax, and read what happened.

Define Excellence

STRATEGIC OBJECTIVE AND METRICS

The first step is to ensure that there is organizational alignment in regard to the strategic objective. In this case, the client's objective was to simply achieve a more efficient and accurate forecasting system, which in turn would improve customer on-time delivery and inventory turns. Based upon this objective, we selected MAPE as the metric to measure progress. Data analysis found that inaccurate forecasts were the chronic issue most impacting on-time delivery to the customer.

As pointed out earlier in the book, the forecast to use for the metric is dependent upon the cumulative product lead time. We estimated that this lead time was about six months. This meant that we compared the actual demand to the forecast that we published six months before.

Case Study

Mine the Gaps

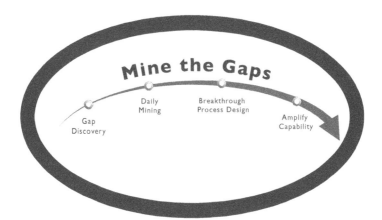

Gap Discovery

Next, it was necessary to assess actual forecast inaccuracies and investigate what caused them. If you analyze enough "defect data," patterns will emerge. We found that the primary cause was inaccuracies in new product forecasts. It was clear from the data that recently introduced new products had severely undersold the forecast. If you have worked in the supply chain world for any amount of time, you will not be surprised by this finding.

Obviously, lack of historical demand makes new product forecasts more challenging. However, it was the slow reaction time that concerned me. From the launch date, it was clear that the new product was not meeting sales projections, yet the client did not reduce the forecast until five months after the launch date.

The sales team did not want to admit defeat initially until it was too difficult to ignore. In this case, the new product forecasts were consistently above actual demand. In other words, significant positive forecast bias existed.

DAILY MINING

Gap Discovery is necessary but not sufficient. It focuses on what happened in the *past*, which makes sense since the past tends to repeat itself. This is especially true if the company has done little to fix the process that caused the problems in the first place. However, it is critical to have a *real-time view* of your supply chain to address issues as they arise.

We developed a Daily Mining process to monitor actual demand versus forecasts. If the customer base had placed large orders the previous day, causing supply shortages, there was still time to intervene and look for alternative solutions. This quick intervention improved results, but the real value was the timely understanding of chronic issues related to forecasts. For example, we soon found a key issue: large unforecasted orders placed by distributors who were simply replenishing safety stock. These orders could cause stockouts for other customers and impact the overall supply chain objective. After we implemented Daily Mining and reviewed large orders, stockouts declined significantly.

BREAKTHROUGH PROCESS DESIGN

Solid supply chain performance results require good people and robust business processes. But which processes? To answer that question, we must answer another: What are the primary outputs of the forecast management process? Remember, a process converts inputs to outputs, so an output is evidence that a process is nearby.

In the table below, I have listed those desired outputs and the associated business processes:

Output	Business Process
Forecasts	Forecast Management Forecast Strategy
Customer orders with accurate commit dates	Customer Order Management Demand Control
Optimal inventory	Safety stock management Inventory strategy Manufacturing strategy
Continual improvement	Root cause analysis Daily Mining

Table 15: Desired outputs and associated processes.

Next, we differentiated between **enabling** and **operational** processes. Enabling processes are the ones that support the operational processes. They tend to be more strategic and completed less frequently. In this case, the enabling processes were:

1. Manufacturing strategy
2. Safety stock management
3. ABC stratification
4. Forecast strategy
5. Root cause analysis

Operational processes are the ones that execute the strategy. A company must manage these processes daily, and they must apply discipline to them. These were the processes that we selected:

1. Forecast management
2. Customer order management
3. Demand control
4. Daily Mining

Lean Forecasting Demystified

It was now necessary to analyze these processes to determine pain points (a.k.a. gaps), which would help inform the future state business process design. Here are some of the key pain points:

Forecast Management

Firstly, the client did not publish the forecast until about two weeks into each quarter. At that time, the finance team would schedule a meeting with sales and operations to define the number of instruments they projected to sell that quarter. The horizon of the forecast was until the end of the same quarter. Its purpose was to predict quarter revenue and not much else.

Nobody could tell me anything about forecast accuracy levels or bias. In other words, on a scale of one to ten, their forecasting capability was about negative five.

In addition, since there were so many more consumable items than instruments, and total consumable revenue was less than instruments, the sales team did not forecast consumable items.

There was not a documented forecast process. What little process existed was consistent from quarter to quarter. The client told me that seasonality existed, but if I asked ten people to explain it to me, I would get eleven different answers.

Inventory Strategy

They had many saleable, consumable finished goods items, but they considered everything to be MTS. This was the case even though many items would expire within four to six months from the manufacture date. What could go wrong? You guessed it, expired inventory was rampant. Unfortunately, they did not consistently input expiration dates into their inventory management system. This meant that many times, they first noticed that a batch had expired when they picked the bottle from the refrigerator and looked at the label. Unfortunately, this was just before they had scheduled the batch for use in production, resulting in the need to delay production runs, often meaning finished goods stockouts and frustrated customers. In fact, their on-time shipment performance to customers was less than fifty percent.

In terms of understanding chronic inventory issues, excess, or shortages, there had been truly little analysis performed. As a result, they regarded key metrics, such as on-time delivery and inventory turns, as a trade-off. They assumed that to improve one, the other had to suffer. In this case, they have managed to improve their on-time delivery to customers by doubling inventory.

Customer Order Management

Customer order management was overly simplistic. There was a standard lead time for each product category that they manually added to the order entry date. This calculated the commit date. Whenever a specific item was backordered, the operations group updated a spreadsheet weekly and sent it to order management. Whenever a customer placed an order for these backordered items, the order management rep was meant to remember that it was on the list and give it a later commit date than the standard lead time. You guessed it—this was frequently forgotten, and they overpromised delivery dates.

To exacerbate the problem, if orders did not ship on time, they did not proactively notify customers, and they did not revise the commit date. This meant lots of frustrated phone calls and emails between the customer, order management, and the operations group.

Future State Process Design

Based upon these findings, we developed the future state business process below that would address many pain points. Note that the numbers in each box are unique, sequential identifiers, and the top of each box shows the software used for that activity.

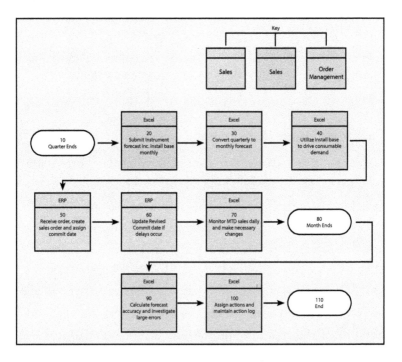

Figure 41: Future state process design.

Case Study

This stage of evolution was clearly still far away from the ideal state, but it was major progress compared to where they started. To achieve this future state, it was necessary to identify all the changes required. Here are some examples of proposed improvements:

- ➤ Create two-quarter forecasts for instruments to enhance visibility to material requirements with enough time to purchase the long lead-time items.

- ➤ Develop a forecast planning BOM for consumables based upon the number of active instruments at customer sites.

- ➤ Use historical demand data to convert quarterly forecasts to monthly forecasts.

- ➤ Hold monthly meetings to discuss forecast changes to modify plans throughout the quarter.

- ➤ Implement two new fields in the ERP system; namely, a revised commit date and request date.

- ➤ Reschedule delayed orders and notify customers of the revised commit date.

- ➤ Record the request date to enable tracking of on-time shipment versus this date.

- ➤ Develop demand control processes to react quickly when actual demand differs from the sales forecast.

- ➤ Designate a Demand Controller who monitors customer orders and calls a meeting with the sales team if necessary.

Lean Forecasting Demystified

> ➤ Establish several key metrics to monitor progress, including forecast MAPE, forecast bias, customer order lead time, and on-time shipment versus request date.

They prioritized these opportunities in the Bridge the Gaps phase.

AMPLIFY CAPABILITY

The last step in the Mine the Gap phase was to assess the client's capability level versus the key Lean Forecasting practices outlined in this book. Below are the results of that assessment, and explanations of the scoring rationale for selected statements.

1= Strongly disagree, 2 = Disagree, 3 = Neutral, 4 = Agree, 5 = Strongly Agree

Item Reduction

Topic	Statement	Score
Independent to dependent demand	Opportunities to convert items to dependent demand have been evaluated and implemented where possible	1
ATO	Assemble to order opportunities have been evaluated and implemented where applicable.	2
Pull	Opportunities to "Pull" versus "Push" have been evaluated and implemented where appropriate	1
Aggregation/ proration	A hierarchy has been established so forecasting can be performed top down, bottom up or middle out	1

Table 16: Assessment: Item Reduction.

ATO

The client does have a quasi-ATO strategy for its consumable kits. Components are kitted together in the warehouse. However, it is inconsistent. Sometimes they maintain a kit inventory, but at other times they do not assemble the kits until the customer places an order. The proposal was to define a robust ATO process.

Pull

There is only "push" and no "pull." There were a few opportunities to implement a pull system and thereby reduce the number of items to forecast. The client sold their flagship instrument in multiple versions. They could remove the need to forecast the options, thus allowing customer orders to drive the instrument version that they assembled.

ABC Stratification

Topic	Statement	Score
ABC stratification	Planners spend roughly 80% of their time on A items, and minimal time on the C items	1
Detailed forecast time fence	Cumulative lead time is understood and utilized to define detailed forecast time fence	1

Table 17: Assessment: ABC stratification.

They had performed ABC stratification, but the criteria used was inventory value. The accounting group had much influence over that decision.

Market Intelligence

Topic	Statement	Score
Forecast strategy selection	An effective process exists for evaluating item demand variability versus volume to select forecast strategy	1
Market Intelligence	An effective process exists for considering market intelligence to help develop the forecast	2
Opportunities/Threats/Assumptions	Demand opportunities, threats and assumptions are quantified and reviewed	1
Forecast Units/Intervals/Horizon	Forecast data includes units, monthly intervals and at least a 12-month horizon	1
Unconstrained forecast	Forecasts are unconstrained by supply limitations	4
Demand influencing	Demand influencing is practiced to manage demand	1
Multiple Series	Forecasts from several sources (statistics, sales, analyst etc.) are tracked	1
Multiple demand sources	All demand sources are included in the forecast, including samples, engineering runs etc.	3

Table 18: Assessment: market intelligence.

They discussed market intelligence in their sales meetings, especially as quarter-end neared. However, it was sporadic, and the horizon was much too short for supply chain needs.

Order Management

Topic	Statement	Score
Order date management	Consensus on definition of key dates related to sales orders (request, original promise, revised promise etc.)	2
Demand control	Demand is controlled to react quickly when actual demand varies significantly from the forecast.	1
ATP	Available to Promise (ATP) functionality works effectively to calculate customer order commit dates	1
Forecast consumption	Forecast consumptions policies have been established and configured in the applicable software	1

Table 19: Assessment: order management.

ATP

ATP functionality did not exist in their ERP system, so it was challenging to accurately commit to projected ship dates. Instead, they had standard lead times for each product type and a list of exceptions updated weekly. Since this was such a manual process, the commit dates were often inaccurate. In fact, their on-time shipping performance versus original commit dates was less than fifty percent.

Forecast Consumption

The client did not manage forecasts in the ERP system, so forecast consumption functionality was not applicable. Instead, they tracked actual demand versus forecasts in spreadsheets, quarter by quarter. In this case, they could only consume forecasts within the quarter. If actual demand exceeded forecasts, they could not consume the forecast for the following quarter. They managed each quarter independently. Similarly, unconsumed forecasts at the end of a quarter did not carry over to the next one.

Unfortunately, the proposal for ATP and forecast consumption would require a new ERP system, which would be at least two years away.

Measurement

Topic	Statement	Score
Forecast Accuracy	A consensus exists for forecast accuracy metric, and it is regarded as a key metric by your organization.	1
Forecast off-set	When calculating forecast accuracy, the cumulative lead time is considered in selecting forecast offset period	1
Demand definition	Alignment of meaning of "demand", considering either order date, request date, ship date etc.	1
Safety stock optimization	Safety stock is optimized using historical demand/ supply lead time variation and desired service level	1
Forecast Bias	Forecast bias is routinely measured, and actions are taken to reduce it where necessary	1
FVA	Forecast Value Added has been evaluated and the process has been modified based upon the results	1
Multiple Series	Forecasts from several sources (statistics, sales, analyst etc.) are tracked	1
Multiple demand sources	All demand sources are included in the forecast, including samples, engineering runs etc.	3

Table 20: Assessment: Measurement.

The client did not have any form of forecast accuracy measurement, so this section was, unfortunately, easy enough to score. In addition, there had been no discussion regarding the definition of demand. Finally, they did not calculate safety stock levels considering demand and lead time variation.

BRIDGE THE GAPS

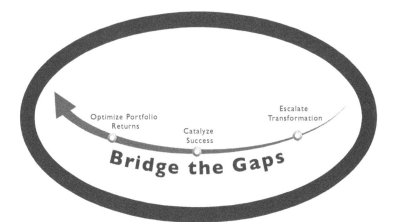

Now that we have performed the assessment, and identified the gaps, it was time to bridge those gaps. But, in a target rich environment, it is easy to become overwhelmed in deciding where to start. In other words, it was necessary to prioritize all the gaps identified so far. In the table below, you can see the results of this assessment.

Prioritization

As in the earlier chapter, prioritization was performed by scoring impact and effort on a scale of 1–5.

Lean Forecasting Demystified

1=Strongly disagree, 2 = Disagree, 3 = Neither agree nor disagree, 4 = Agree, 5 = Strongly Agree

Topic	Statement	Impact	Effort	Phase 1 (Y/N)
ATO	Assemble to order opportunities have been evaluated and implemented where applicable.	3	5	N
Pull	Opportunities to "Pull" versus "Push" have been evaluated and implemented where appropriate	4	5	N
ABC stratification	Planners spend roughly 80% of their time on A items, and minimal time on the C items	4	2	Y
Market Intelligence	An effective process exists for considering market intelligence to help develop the forecast	3	2	Y
Forecast Units/Intervals/Horizon	Forecast data includes units, monthly intervals and at least a 12-month horizon	5	2	Y
Order date management	Consensus on definition of key dates related to sales orders (request, original promise, revised promise etc.)	3	3	Y
Demand control	Demand is controlled to react quickly when actual demand varies significantly from the forecast.	5	2	Y
ATP	Available to Promise (ATP) functionality works effectively to calculate customer order commit dates	4	4	N
Forecast consumption	Forecast consumptions policies have been established and configured in the applicable software	2	5	N
Forecast Accuracy	A consensus exists for forecast accuracy metric, and it is regarded as a key metric by your organization.	5	3	Y
Forecast off-set	When calculating forecast accuracy, the cumulative lead time is considered in selecting forecast offset period	4	2	Y
Forecast Bias	Forecast bias is routinely measured, and actions are taken to reduce it where necessary	5	2	Y

Table 21: Prioritizing the gaps.

176

Based upon the results, we worked with the client to select what would be included in Phase 1 (noted in the last column). Those opportunities that scored *high impact* and *low effort* (a.k.a. low hanging fruit) were high priority and included in Phase 1. For the opportunities with *high impact* and *high effort* (a.k.a. projects), we were judicious about which ones to include in the first phase. It was important not to overwhelm the organization and cause the whole initiative to fail. As you can see below, the highest effort rating included in Phase 1 was a "3," whereas they added all items with a "2" rating to the scope of the first phase.

RESULTS

We started to see improvements almost immediately. On-time shipping performance was typically below fifty percent previously and average lead times were about seventeen calendar days, so it was a pretty low hurdle. However, nobody predicted that the average lead time would reduce to six days within a quarter. At the same time, the client's ability to meet their original commitments rose dramatically to about ninety-four percent.

In terms of forecast accuracy, the previous forecasting method achieved a twenty-nine percent MAPE score, and they soon improved this to twenty-two percent. We should also remember that the previous forecasting method only published forecasts within the current quarter, whereas the new forecast metric used a six-month lag to allow for material lead times. In other words, the new method performed much better even with a major handicap.

To confirm that the forecasting process was now adding value, we calculated the naive forecast by simply using sales from the same month as the previous quarter. The naive forecast had an error rate of thirty-three percent. This confirmed that the previous method improved forecast accuracy a little, but the new method was dramatically better than the naive forecast.

Chapter 15

Recap

To improve is to change; to be perfect is to change often.

—Winston Churchill, former UK prime minister

At the start of the book, I promised that I would provide the tools and know-how to eliminate or at least minimize waste in your forecasting process. In this chapter, I will recap the tools covered in this book and how they help removal of each type of waste.

Defects

By employing the tools and practices outlined in this book, we will reduce defects and errors. But first, how do we avoid chasing mice when there are tigers afoot? In other words, unless we use the correct data for forecast accuracy measurements, we could come to the wrong conclusions. We could determine that forecasts are accurate when they are not, and vice versa. For example, we must select the correct forecast offset period and accurately define when demand actually occurred.

Ideally, your organization would track the accuracy of forecasts from various sources, such as sales team, S&OP, statistical forecasts, modified forecasts, etc. By monitoring these different demand series, over time it will become clear which are the most accurate sources. Now that we are using the correct data to measure accuracy and the best forecast source, we can identify the most chronic reason for causes of forecast error.

But beware: the most dangerous tigers are often senior executives. Firstly, management often sets unrealistic forecast accuracy targets that do not consider demand volatility. This can cause us to waste our time striving to achieve a target that is unachievable. Since we are picking on senior management, determine whether their meddling has created forecast bias, which increases unnecessary inaccuracies.

My final words on management are more positive. Their most important contribution to forecast accuracy is the removal of artificial volatility. This will render the forecaster's job much easier as demand becomes more stable.

Although I have extolled the virtues of minimizing items to forecast, there can be a point of diminishing returns. It is important to strike the right balance between aggregating forecasts to reduce the effort required but not aggregating so much that you lose important demand patterns.

Effective management of the customer order entry process will also greatly impact defect levels. For example, do you consume forecasts appropriately when you create sales orders? If not, you could inadvertently increase or lower the demand that is driving your supply planning process. In addition, do you tag abnormal demand, such as sales promotions or stocking warehouses, when you launch a new product? If not, then this will skew historical demand utilized to calculate forecasts.

Overproduction

In the forecasting context, overproduction refers to how many items we forecast. An MTS strategy could cause this, while an ATO strategy would be more effective. This is especially true if item demand is low and volatility high. In addition, your organization forecasts items that have dependent demand.

Many companies do not understand how far into the future they must forecast at the item level. In this case, it could be an unnecessarily long time before they switch from item to product family forecasts. Finally, overproduction can also be related to user software requirements. When an organization announces a new forecasting software, it is not unusual for users to request more functional requirements than the company can realistically digest.

Extra Processing

This waste is frequently caused by organizations that do not provide usable forecasts. This could include forecasts that are revenue-only and have large intervals over an abbreviated time horizon with insufficient detail (i.e., over-aggregated). Somebody must rework a forecast whenever it is missing key information.

As we all know, system transactions are not always user-friendly, causing unnecessary processing. Software functionality gaps or an ineffective implementation of the software can cause this.

Finally, if a company has not selected an appropriate strategy, then there will always be extra processing. For example, if a popular item has low volatility, then statistical forecasting could be a good option. However, if you decide instead to attempt to collaborate with a large customer, then you might be wasting your time. Since demand volatility is already low, it is likely that a statistical forecast will be more accurate than your customer.

Inventory

The forecasting process, or lack thereof, can cause excessive inventory levels. For example, we should centralize storage of low demand (C) items into fewer DCs. Having a suboptimal inventory deployment strategy could cause excess inventory at multiple DCs, which will be difficult to forecast for these C items. We should optimize safety stock levels based upon several factors including demand variability. In the absence of the scientific approach, organizations tend to stock more than needed—the archetypal "just in case" inventory due to lack of confidence in manual safety stock calculations.

Pull inventory management systems put a cap on the maximum inventory level for any given item, based upon the number of kanbans and kanban quantity. On the other hand, push systems have no such limit, and so tend to create much more inventory than necessary.

Transportation

Transportation in the context of forecasting refers to the waste associated with excessive hand-offs between departments. For example, multiple stakeholders make modifications before they publish the forecast, even though there is evidence to suggest that these modifications do not improve accuracy. This issue suggests that we should redesign the forecasting process to remove unnecessary hand-offs and approvals.

Underutilized people

Unfortunately, employees often do not feel empowered to make decisions. For example, senior management may have given the demand planner a forecast that the planner knows is unrealistic, but they feel powerless to share their opinion.

Although forecasting leverages statistical quantitative techniques, information held by employees is vital. This can include market intelligence from the sales team or untapped knowledge held by the customer. Most organizations publish forecasts as a single number, with no other information. But the forecast might include potential new accounts that may not transpire, thus causing a risk. Alternatively, the sales team may have decided to omit this information from the forecast, and so there is an opportunity. It would be helpful to understand these risks or opportunities, which could cause the supply chain team to make hugely different decisions. For example, say the sales team has a meeting scheduled in two weeks with a potential new customer. If they were aware, the supply chain team could hold off on making large commitments for two weeks.

Motion

Here we are referring to the amount of effort spent on forecasting specific items. ABC categorization can help decide where to focus your attention. As discussed earlier, **20 percent of your items account for 80 percent of total demand (A items),** so it is wise to give them most of your attention. Alternatively, half of your items only account for 5 percent of total demand, so if you have not categorized your product portfolio, it is possible that you are wasting 50 percent of your time.

Your organization could also be forecasting at a suboptimal level of your product hierarchy. For example, you are forecasting at the item-DC level, when you could actually be forecasting at the item level. You can use a forecast planning BOM to distribute the forecast to DCs, thus exponentially reducing forecasting efforts.

Waiting

Whenever a company does not perform actions in a timely manner, they suffer the waste of waiting. This could include waiting for all demand sources or customers waiting for their delayed orders to become available. There could be delays in the reaction time to obvious issues, such as actual sales differing dramatically from the forecast. At a more strategic level, it might be that management has not been willing to prune their product portfolio, increasing the number of items that require a forecast. Finally, waiting could refer to incomplete user requirements for forecasting software, which could impact whether we select the best solution.

Epilogue

Anyone who thinks that they are too small to make a difference has never tried to fall asleep with a mosquito in the room.

—The Dalai Lama, Nobel Peace Prize recipient

Competitive Advantage

After reading the manuscript for this book, one of my editors, who has only a basic understanding of supply chain management, asked me if all these stories were true. She was having a hard time believing that critical practices were managed so incompetently in large organizations. When I assured her that they were, she admitted to being shocked. I must confess that earlier in my career, I had the same reaction. Even though supply chain management now receives more attention, I have not yet noticed an improved awareness or understanding of best practices. I believe that many organizations still regard supply chain as tactical and have not yet become serious about mastering its disciplines.

My theory is that almost all other functions, such as finance, IT, engineering, and legal, require employees to hold specialized certifications and degrees to be considered qualified for professional jobs within that field. On the other hand, supply chain has a lower barrier to entry. It is possible to fulfill all its functions without directly related education. However, excelling within supply chain requires a deep understanding of the principles, concepts, and practices. For example, the most fundamental question in supply chain may be when we must place another order with our supplier to prevent a stockout and to avoid excess inventory. This is known as the reorder point. I asked my network, "What are the three variables required to calculate this critical value?" It was a multiple- choice poll with four options, and they had to select the one that was *not* part of the reorder point formula. From 284 responses, sixty percent were correct. In a review of the incorrect respondents, almost all were supply chain professionals, many in senior positions, with MBAs and supply chain certifications. Since nobody was required to respond, I assume that the respondents felt more confident than the non-respondents, which makes me think that the total network would have achieved a lower score.

My point is that understanding even the supply chain basics will give you a competitive advantage in the marketplace. The fact that you read this book suggests that you recognize the importance of learning and that you are motivated to do so. If you plan to apply your newfound knowledge within your firm, then it is your organization that has gained this competitive advantage.

10 Takeaways

Below are 10 points that I believe are the most critical to remember when embarking upon your Lean Forecasting journey. They are in order of importance, based upon my opinion (not some scientific study):

1. Begin with a positive mindset and assume that there are many opportunities in your organization to adopt Lean Forecasting practices.

2. Have zero tolerance for forecast bias. It is induced by bad management practice.

3. Leverage the 80/20 rule to focus on a few critical items.

4. Leverage the Law of Large Numbers to achieve higher forecast accuracy with less effort.

5. Lead with common-sense tools, not complicated technology.

6. Implement no software until a high degree of data accuracy is achieved (garbage in, garbage out).

7. Aim for forecasts that are at least more accurate than the naive version.

8. Adopt a winning strategy by reducing artificial volatility.

9. Ensure that forecast accuracy targets reflect demand volatility. Hope is not a strategy.

10. Understand that humans tend to overreact to perceived patterns (pareidolia), resulting in more forecast error.

When I reflect upon this list, the clear message is that people must understand where their approach is harming the forecasting process. It also tells me that instead of a premature reliance on technology, we should take time to understand some of these key principles, such as the 80/20 rule, LLN, GIGO, artificial volatility, naive forecasts, and pareidolia. I believe that this approach is a major departure from current practice. In my experience, the focus is on the shiny new technology that will transform your supply chain, with its 382 different statistical forecast methods. I apologize to my friends who rely upon continued software sales for their livelihoods. If I don't receive a Christmas card this year, I completely understand. But, as the saying goes, "If the only tool you have is a hammer, then you tend to see every problem as a nail."

To be clear, I am not opposed to technology when introduced at the appropriate time. I'm opposed to the premature introduction of technology, resulting in frustration, false hopes, wasted resources, and failed implementations.

The good news is that you now have the necessary tools. You are empowered to transform your forecasting system. Where progress requires support from above your pay grade, then advocate for a Lean approach to forecasting. Clearly, everybody wants a more accurate forecast achieved with less effort, in which case, the key gap is insufficient understanding of these powerful practices within your organization.

1. Determine if there is forecast bias, and if so, raise visibility and demonstrate how it negatively impacts your supply chain and how it can be addressed.

2. Calculate naive forecast accuracy and set that as the minimum target. If you discover that your forecast has more errors than the naive version, then communicate this fact within your organization.

3. Identify high volume items that also have excessive volatility. It is highly probable that a large portion of this volatility is artificial. Investigate the reasons for high volatility and strive to remove it.

4. Obtain data for different forecast versions, especially where people have modified the original forecast.

Determine if these modifications are positively or negatively impacting accuracy. If it is the latter, then find a tactful way to communicate these findings to minimize these unnecessary alterations in the future.

5. Initiate the Mine the Gaps approach as outlined in Chapter 14. This data-driven, structured approach will be the fastest way not only to achieve quick wins but also long-term, sustained transformation.

I hope that you enjoyed learning about Lean Forecasting as much as I did. I believe that it will be as beneficial to your organization and career as it was to mine. Now, your next challenge will be what to do with all your newfound spare time.

Bibliography

Box, George E. P. "Robustness in the strategy of scientific model building." Robustness in Statistics. Edited by Robert L. Launer and Graham N. Wilkinson. 1979. New York: Academic Press.

Brown, Peter Jensen. "History and Etymology of 'Happy Hour.'" Early Sports and Pop Culture History Blog. April 2, 2014. https://esnpc.blogspot.com/2014/04/history-and-etymology-of-happy-hour.html.

Dick, Steven J. and Keith L. Cowing, editors. "Risk and Exploration: Earth, Sea and the Stars." NASA Administrator's Symposium. September 26-29, 2004. https://history.arc.nasa.gov/hist_pdfs/book_risk+explore/riskandexploration_all.pdf.

Gartner. "Gartner for Supply Chain: Strengthening Supply Chain Performance Improvement Initiatives." Gartner. 2021. https://www.scribd.com/document/650044505/Gartner-Hierarchy-Supply-Chain-Metrics-Benchmarking.

Holmes, David, Todd Ferguson, and Timm Reiher. "Demand Control: An Often Missing link in a Demand Management Process." Oliver Wight Americas. October 10, 2019. https://www.oliverwight-americas.com/whitepapers/demand-control/.

Karelse, Jonathon. "How to Improve Forecast Performance by Reducing Human Bias." LinkedIn. May 14, 2019. https://www.linkedin.com/pulse/how-improve-forecast-performance-reducing-human-bias-jonathon-karelse/.

Microsoft Support. "BESSELI function." Microsoft. Accessed June 10, 2024. https://support.microsoft.com/en-us/office/besseli-function-8d33855c-9a8d-444b-98e0-852267b1c0df.

NASA, Viking 1. Face on Mars. July 25, 1976. Accessed on July 9, 2024. https://www.esa.int/ESA_Multimedia/Images/2006/09/Face_on_Mars_illusion_as_seen_by_Viking_1

Steutermann, Steven. "Win the Business Case for Investment to Improve Forecast Accuracy." Gartner. 2017. https://www.gartner.com/document/3701817.

Recommended Reading

Chapman, Steve, Tony Arnold, Ann Gatewood and Lloyd Clive. *Introduction to Materials Management.* Pearson, 8th Edition. 2016.

Clarke, Steve. *Mine the Gaps.* Publish Your Purpose. 2023.

Crumm, Colleen and George Palmatier. *Demand Management Best Practices.* J. Ross Publishing. 2003.

Gilliland, Michael. *The Business Forecasting Deal.* Wiley. 2010.

Hammer, Michael and James Champy. *Reengineering the Corporation.* Harper Collins. 2009.

King, Peter L. "Crack the Code." APICS Magazine. July/August 2011. http://media.apics.org/omnow/Crack%20the%20Code.pdf.

Liker, Jeffrey K. *The Toyota Way.* McGraw Hill. 2006.

Sandras, William A. Jr. *Just-in-Time: Making it Happen.* Wiley Press, 2008.

Shook, John. *Managing to Learn.* Lean Enterprises Institute. 2008.

Vandeput, Nicolas. *Demand Forecasting Best Practices.* Manning. 2023.

Wallace, Thomas F. and Robert A. Stahl. *Sales Forecasting, A New Approach.* 2002.

Womack, James P., Daniel T. Jones, and Daniel Roos. *The Machine that Changed the World.* Free Press. 2007.

Acknowledgments

I'd like to start by thanking my mum and dad for their hard work in raising four kids and scraping enough money together for a quality education and all the opportunities that sprang from that.

Next, I must thank the manager at ICI, Manchester, who encouraged me to go back to school after a few weeks working on a Youth Training Scheme. You encouraged me to take a path that transformed my life.

I'm grateful to my good friend, Brian White, for all the great diagrams in this book.

Thank you to the good people at Publish Your Purpose, especially Alexander Loutsenko for keeping me on track and Brandi Lai for your help in the editing process.

Last, but not least, my lovely wife for believing in me and providing the support, without which this book would not have been possible.

Index

Page numbers in italics refer to figures and tables.

ABC stratification,
Abnormal demand,
Absolute difference,
Aggregation,
Agile,
Amplify capability,
Artificial volatility,
Assemble-to-order (ATO),
Available-to-promise,
Benchmarks,
Bias,
Bill: of materials,
  of resource,
Breakthrough process design,
Bridge the Gaps,
Buckets,
Business process,
Capable-to-promise,
Capacity planning,
Catalyze success,
Commit dates,
Constrained,
Cumulative lead time,
Current state,

Customer: collaboration,
  order management,
Daily mining,
Defect data,
Demand: control,
  date,
  planning,
  shaping,
  sources,
  variability,
  versus supply,
  volatility,
  volume,
Dependent demand items,
Disaggregation,
Dynamic safety stock,
Enterprise resource planning (ERP),
Escalate transformation,
Fill-in jobs,
Forecast: accuracy,
  consumption,
  details,
  offset,

planning bill of material (FPBOM),

series,

strategy,

value-added (FVA),

Future state,

Gap Discovery,

Garbage In, Garbage Out (GIGO),

Gartner,

Hierarchies,

Human intervention,

Inherent volatility,

Interval,

Inventory deployment strategy,

Kanban,

Law of Large Numbers (LLN),

Long-term planning,

Make-to-order (MTO),

Make-to-stock (MTS),

Manual adjustments,

Manufacturing strategy,

Market intelligence,

Master production schedule,

Material requirements planning,

Mean absolute deviation (MAD),

Mean absolute percent error (MAPE),

Mine the Gaps,

Minimum: order quantity (MOQ),

remaining shelf life (MRSL),

viable product (MVP),

Min-Max,

Moving average,

Multiple series,

Naive forecast,

negative bias,

Opportunities,

Optimal portfolio returns,

Order entry date,

Pareto principle,

Positive bias,

Prioritization,

Product families,

Projects,

Quick wins,

Reorder point,

Request dates,

Risks,

Root cause analysis,

Rough-cut capacity planning,

Running sum of forecast error (RSFE),

Sales: and Operations Planning,

incentives,

Seasonality,

Service level,

Index

Ship date,
SKU pruning,
Software requirements,
Standard deviation,
Statistical forecasting,
Stock keeping unit,
Stockouts,
Strategic: objective,
    planning,
    roadmap,
Supply planning,
Targets,

Thankless tasks,
Time: fence,
   horizon,
Tracking signal,
Unconstrained,
Unit of measure,
Unscheduled repairs,
User requirements,
Value-added,
Volume versus Mix,
Waste,
Z score,

Types of Waste

DEFECTS

Practice	Waste
Abnormal demand	Not captured
Artificial volatility	Excessive
Commit dates	Inaccurate
Customer order dates	Inaccurate
Demand date	Incorrect
Demand shaping	Insufficient
Demand versus supply	Imbalanced
Demand volatility	Excessive
Forecast	Inaccurate
Forecast	Biased
Forecast accuracy targets	Arbitrary
Forecast offset	Insufficient
Forecast series	Insufficient
Mean absolute percent error (MAPE)	Excessive
Request dates	Inaccurate
Running sum of forecast error (RSFE)	Excessive
Targets	Inappropriate
Tracking signal	Not captured

OVERPRODUCTION

Dependent demand items	Forecasted
Forecast mix	Excessive
Make-to-stock	Unnecessary
Pull versus push	Imbalanced
Time horizon	Excessive

EXTRA PROCESSING

Forecast	Constrained
Forecast strategy	Suboptimal
Forecast tactics	Suboptimal
Interval size	Excessive
Naive forecast	Not communicated
Software	Ineffective
Software requirements	Excessive
Time horizon	Insufficient
Unit of measure	Incorrect

INVENTORY

Inventory availability	Inaccurate
Inventory deployment strategy	Suboptimal
Manufacturing strategy	Suboptimal
Reorder point	Inaccurate
Safety stocks	Suboptimal
Seasonality	Not captured
Stockouts	Excessive

Types of Waste

TRANSPORTATION
Business process	Undefined
Forecast value added	Insufficient
Manual forecast changes	Excessive
Underutilized People	
Customer collaboration	Insufficient
Forecast assumptions	Not communicated
Market intelligence	Not communicated
Opportunities	Not communicated
Risk	Not communicated
Motion	
ABC stratification	Insufficient
Aggregation	Suboptimal
Agile Project Management	Insufficient
Forecast details	Excessive
Pareto principle	Underutilization

WAITING
Daily Mining	Insufficient
Demand controls	Insufficient
Demand sources	Incomplete
Forecast details	Insufficient
Order rescheduling	Delayed
Quick wins	Insufficient
Reaction time	Delayed
SKU pruning	Delayed
Software	Misaligned
Software requirements	Incomplete

The Authority on Supply Chain Strategy

Steve Clarke is the founder of BioSupply Consulting LLC, which helps life science organizations transform their supply chain capability and performance. He has been the guest speaker at several APICS events and supply chain related podcasts. He also publishes a weekly newsletter to his 16K LinkedIn followers.

With over 25 years of industry experience and unmatched expertise, and a deep passion for supply chain solutions, Steve Clarke has helped numerous clients – from small start-ups to major life science companies – solve chronic problems and achieve strategic objects.

His journey in supply management began right after college and, after obtaining his BS in Biochemistry at the University of Sheffield, England and an MBA from CSU East Bay, he rose to an executive position at Jacuzzi Inc. by the age of 33. Now, as a well-known and trusted consultant, executives turn to him to transform their supply chain performance and capabilities.

Over the years, he has developed an unparalleled reputation for his structured approach, tenacity, and his ability to consistently deliver results.

Steve's enthusiasm for what he does means he is equally comfortable discussing strategy with the C-Suite as I am explaining kanban to shop floor employees. He doesn't just deliver a slide deck: he works alongside you, ensuring practical implementation and real results.

For every engagement, Steve will gather your requirements, design, develop, and implement proven solutions tailored to your needs. He will work with you to elevate your supply chain to new heights!

If you would like to learn more about how to quickly and sustainably transform supply chain performance for your patients, customers, and other stakeholders, please email Steve at steve@biosupplyconsulting.com, or check out his work at biosupplyconsulting.com.

Get in Touch

Website
biosupplconsulting.com

Linkedin
https://www.linkedin.com/in/steve-clarke1

Email
steve@biosupplyconsulting.com

Did you like Lean Forecasting Demystified?

**Delve even deeper with Steve's first book,
Mine the Gaps, available now!**

In today's dynamic and high-stakes business landscape, companies are in continual pursuit of strategies to boost productivity, curtail wasteful efforts, and achieve greater effectiveness, efficiency, and profitability. Teams are constantly under scrutiny of performance metrics and systems meant to underpin objectives to support company goals. Anticipated challenges stemming from exponential growth and unforeseen disruptions such as a global pandemic put strain on even the most robust and seemingly well working systems, exposing flawed systems and growth opportunities for all, supply chains included.

What should you do when your organization is on the verge of outgrowing its processes and capabilities? What can you do when band-aids holding supply chain systems in place are losing their stronghold? And, more importantly, how can you proactively prevent or mitigate supply chain issues?

In *Mine the Gaps*, Steve Clarke, an experienced professional in the field of life science supply chain operations, shares invaluable insights into his tried-and-true methodology to prevent common supply chain issues with effective process design and execution. Drawing from years of hands-on experience, Clarke understands that when things feel chaotic and out of control, it's essential to focus on what is within your span of control. And one of the most powerful tools at your disposal is a well-defined framework for identifying gaps and bridging them, transforming your business operations, supply chain processes, and business outcomes along the way.

Too often businesses waste time on scorecards, dashboards, and analytics that provide them with little or no insight. Clarke reveals how to leverage readily available data that will result in quick wins and select relevant metrics that are actionable and drive better business decisions.

In *Mine the Gaps*, readers can expect to:

- ➤ Learn 7 process redesign principles that will transform how work gets done
- ➤ Uncover pitfalls to avoid and how to put measures in place for prevention efforts
- ➤ Explore a tested and realistic roadmap for companies to leverage and tailored to their specific needs

Clarke underscores the notion that process improvement and operational innovation are key drivers of superior outcomes. Through actionable insights, real-world examples, and proven strategies to help overcome challenges and achieve supply chain excellence, *Mine the Gaps* offers a powerful and comprehensive framework that empowers businesses to achieve supply chain excellence and organizational success. Unlock the full potential of your supply chain, optimize operations, and position yourself at the forefront of your industry.

Get your copy now!

The B Corp Movement

Dear reader,

Thank you for reading this book and joining the Publish Your Purpose community! You are joining a special group of people who aim to make the world a better place.

What's Publish Your Purpose About?
Our mission is to elevate the voices often excluded from traditional publishing. We intentionally seek out authors and storytellers with diverse backgrounds, life experiences, and unique perspectives to publish books that will make an impact in the world.

Certified

(B)

Corporation

Beyond our books, we are focused on tangible, action-based change. As a woman- and LGBTQ+-owned company, we are committed to reducing inequality, lowering levels of poverty, creating a healthier environment, building stronger communities, and creating high-quality jobs with dignity and purpose.

As a Certified B Corporation, we use business as a force for good. We join a community of mission-driven companies building a more equitable, inclusive, and sustainable global economy. B Corporations must meet high standards of transparency, social and environmental performance, and accountability as determined by the nonprofit B Lab. The certification process is rigorous and ongoing (with a recertification requirement every three years).

How Do We Do This?
We intentionally partner with socially and economically disadvantaged businesses that meet our sustainability goals. We embrace and encourage our authors and employee's differences in race, age, color, disability, ethnicity, family or marital status, gender identity or expression, language, national origin, physical and mental ability, political affiliation, religion, sexual orientation, socio-economic status, veteran status, and other characteristics that make them unique.

Community is at the heart of everything we do—from our writing and publishing programs to contributing to social enterprise nonprofits like reSET (www.resetco.org) and our work in founding B Local Connecticut.

We are endlessly grateful to our authors, readers, and local community for being the driving force behind the equitable and sustainable world we are building together.

To connect with us online or publish with us, visit us at www.publishyourpurpose.com.

Elevating Your Voice,

Jenn T Grace

Jenn T. Grace
Founder, Publish Your Purpose

Printed in the USA
CPSIA information can be obtained
at www.ICGtesting.com
LVHW010953061124
795748LV00019B/335